AMERICAN HERITAGE

February, 1968 · Volume XIX, Number 2

Essay: One-Way Ticket to Oblivion   By PETER LYON

Without the American railroads there could have been no American business. With a web of rails we bound our continental spaces together and spurred them into production; on a skeleton of rails we fleshed out our commerce and hardened our industrial muscles. It is not too much to say that the railroads hauled an underdeveloped nation out of debt and carried it much of the way toward industrial supremacy in the world.

The men who administered the affairs of the railroads were lordly fellows who acknowledged or flouted the law as it fitted their convenience, who trafficked in congressmen like so many chattels, who dangled state legislatures like seals from their watch fobs, who took it for granted that the U.S. Army would squash any strike by their workmen, and who deigned in their spare time to instruct Presidents in the conduct of national affairs.

By 1905, when the American railroads were only seventy-five years old, no other industry approached them in capital investment, in revenues, or in power. A competent observer estimated that their officers controlled one sixth of the wealth of the United States and that their capital was "ten times that of the combined banks and trust companies of the country."

But in the sixty years since then, while the national economy has steadily expanded, the fortunes of the railroads, except in wartime, have as steadily shrunk. During the late 1930's, several railroad companies gave up the struggle and raced to see which might first be run through the wringer of bankruptcy; these companies operated one third of the nation's total mileage of railroad tracks. Many other companies contrived to avert receivership only by virtue of fat federal loans.

The railroads can no longer be usefully measured against other industries. Today there are several corporations (General Motors, Standard Oil of New Jersey, and American Telephone and Telegraph), each of which boasts greater revenues than the entire railroad industry, and each of which

clears a net profit that puts the net profit of the entire railroad industry to shame. Today the railroads haul less than half the nation's freight and only a ludicrous three per cent of its passengers—fewer people than travel by automobile, by airplane, by bus, fewer than by any other mode of public transportation.

What has happened to the railroads? In 1905 they were ogres, feared and detested, collectively portrayed as an octopus or as a school of man-eating sharks. Today they seem to be more like a kitten, not a playful kitten with claws that can scratch, but a poor, bedraggled kitten that has fallen down a well and mews and whimpers piteously to be pulled out.

What has become of the railroad executives who once swaggered about, entertaining Presidents and senators in their private cars? Today they have forsaken their own railroads, preferring to travel on airplanes, for after all, they still deem themselves men of consequence for whom every millisecond is a matter of transcendent importance. Today they snivel in the public market place, begging state governors for a free handout.

It is an extraordinary transformation and, as might be expected, the spokesmen for the railroads, who have had a long period of leisure in which to scratch their heads and puzzle over the matter, know just whom to blame for what they insist is a national crisis in transportation. They have levelled a whole fistful of accusing fingers: at the Interstate Commerce Commission; at their employees, the members of the railroad brotherhoods; at their competitors, the automobile, the airplane, the bus, the truck, the barge, and the pipeline; but first, last, and always most passionately, at the federal government.

That there is a modicum of truth in these plaints must be admitted; not much, to be sure, but enough to measure on a torsion balance.

For example, the Interstate Commerce Commission, which regulates the railroads, affords a fair example of

how successive Congresses, in their infinite wisdom, can contrive a truly impressive bureaucratic snarl. In 1887 the commission comprised five commissioners and a staff not much bigger. In response to "the public necessity and convenience," the commission has bloated up to eleven commissioners and a secretariat of nearly 2,500 persons; the law under which it operates has swollen from a lean statute of ten pages to one of more than four hundred pages; its responsibilities have multiplied like bunnies, and so have its regulations; today its procedures are labyrinthine in method and glacial in dispatch. But if the railroads are to some extent hobbled by regulations dating from the days when a spittoon was still a useful and elegant accessory in the depot, the officers of the railroads have themselves cannily opposed revision or repeal of some of those regulations. And if, on matters of substance, the commission has been known to waver and wobble for as long as nine years before making up its collective mind what it should do, this bureaucratic indecision had its origin, once again, in the conference rooms of the great railroads.

But the railroad men reserve most of their indignation for the government policy that has allocated vast sums of public funds (*i.e.,* taxpayers' money) for the construction of airports, highways, and inland waterways, and for research to improve the technology of aviation and motor transport. In the last twenty years, federal, state, and local governments (*i.e.,* the taxpayers) have spent some two hundred billion dollars on highways, cloverleafs, overpasses, underpasses, tunnels, and bridges for the use of automobiles, trucks, and buses. More billions have gone for airports, air navigation systems, and subsidies to companies operating helicopters.

The anguish of the railroad executive may be imagined. No wonder, say the railroad men, that their freight revenues have dwindled and their passenger revenues all but disappeared.

Moreover, the railroad companies are obliged to pay taxes on their tracks, depots, and other real estate, while highways, airports, and waterways get off scot free.

Isn't it scandalous, and a shame?

Well, no; or, at most, not much.

There is nothing new about federal assistance to those who would travel to and fro. The sovereign power of the United States of America, pursuant to Article I, Section 8, paragraph 3 of the Constitution thereof, has been aiding and abetting private enterprise to stimulate transportation between and among the several states ever since 1802, when Congress appropriated money for the building of the Cumberland Road.

If there is one mode of transportation whose way was smoothed by public funds and by grants of public lands, it is the railroad. The iron horse was fed and watered at the public trough for more than fifty years. No man knows precisely how much of the public's funds was handed over to the railroad promoters by one or another set of politicians; a conservative student of the matter estimated that by 1870 the states alone had given $228,-500,000 in cash, while another $300,-000,000 had been paid over by counties and municipalities. The federal government and the various states gave, in addition, about 184,000,000 acres of the public lands to the railroads; this represents nearly one tenth of the land area of the continental United States. To this day several railroad companies are profitable concerns thanks only to those land grants. Some companies are making more money by exploiting the mineral rights in the lands given them seventy-five years ago than they are by operating their railroads.

In the sweet spirit of conciliation, however, let us suppose that the railroad men are right: they are fettered by archaic regulations and they are harshly and inequitably treated by an arbitrary, exigent government. Good. Let us postulate a sinister plot by a government probably socialist, certainly creeping toward socialism, the leaders of which have sworn to bring the railroads to their knees. But can even such a paranoid fantasy begin to explain the long, steady decline of the railroad industry from its pre-eminence fifty or sixty years ago?

Here is a puzzle. For it is a fact that the railroad is a remarkably efficient form of transportation, and why its operators have not easily, even derisively, squelched their competition is hard to see.

A railroad is a device for rolling people or commodities from one place to another. When it comes to rolling many people in a short time, as in hauling commuters to a city, the railroad is incomparably superior to all other such devices: cheaper, quicker, safer, cleaner, quieter; it needs less real estate and fewer operators to do the job; it can keep rolling in fair weather or foul. On *one* track, a railroad can haul fifty thousand persons an hour. To haul the same number in the same time over a highway requires ten thousand cars travelling in *four* lanes and requires further that the weather be fair, that there be no accidents or mechanical breakdowns, and that each driver carry four passengers.

When it comes to rolling commodities, the railroads' competitive edge is even more startling. A diesel train averages 192 ton-miles to the gallon of fuel, while a truck gets only 58 ton-miles to the gallon. But perhaps the most telling advantage of the railroad lies in manpower. A train hauling one hundred freight cars has a crew of five. To haul a comparable load by truck takes hundreds of drivers.

Nevertheless, the railroads' share of freight revenues has steadily declined. There are some categories of freight (the products of mines, the products of forests) that have traditionally been considered a captive property of the railroads. Yet even here the tonnage is down, the revenues are down.

From first to last, it is a remarkable phenomenon. The men who run the railroads seem to have positively booted the commuters, and the passengers generally, away from their ticket windows and off their trains. They seem to have totally ignored the shippers of freight or to have taken them too much for granted.

Their plant dwindles. "There is much surplus railroad mileage in this country today," Stuart T. Saunders said in 1962. (Mr. Saunders is chairman of the board of the Pennsylvania Railroad, the biggest in the country.) When a railroad company rips up a mile of track, it stands to gain as much as five thousand dollars in cash for salvaged material and will annually save three thousand dollars in maintenance costs and as much as two thousand in taxes. Moreover, the land can then be profitably sold, perhaps to the government (*i.e.*, to the taxpayers) for use as a highway, after which the press agents for the railroad can complain bitterly about tax-free competition from trucks, buses, and automobiles. The total mileage of track diminishes steadily, from 430,000 in 1930 to less than 373,000 today.

Their industry's share of the gross national product dwindles, too. In 1930 railroad revenues accounted for 5.9 per cent of the gross national product; in 1966 they accounted for only 1.4 per cent.

Enough of these somber statistics. The picture seems plain enough: a giant industry, vital to the national economy, has for a half century been on the skids to—what? Receivership? Bankruptcy? Nationalization? The signal blocks ahead are hard to make out.

Any examination of the strange and foolish plight of the railroads will uncover vaulting ambition, dumb luck, sly cunning, gross stupidity, incomprehensible arrogance, and naked greed—in short, all the characteristics that have caused the American to be so universally loved and admired. One further statistic, however, emphasizes the curious contradictions inherent in the industry: despite the fact that the railroads seemed to have been staggering along on very unsteady pins, in 1966 their shareholders were paid $502,000,000 in cash dividends, the highest in the industry's history.

One reason for the current plight of the railroads is their self-defeating policy toward passengers, which Mr. Lyon examines in detail starting on page 52. This essay and the article are from his To Hell in a Day Coach: An Exasperated Look at American Railroads, *to be published this month by J. B. Lippincott Company.*

Center stage in this symbolic chromolithograph of 1909 is occupied by the rail-road—specifically, by a high-stepping locomotive pulling a string of passenger cars. And fittingly enough, for in 1909 long-distance passenger travel in all-steel Pullmans, which had just been introduced, had an aura of glamour now sadly tarnished. Trolleys have nearly disappeared, of course, and giant ocean liners seem to be on their way out: Cunard retired the **Queen Mary** *last year and the* **Queen Elizabeth** *will sail off into the sunset this fall. Obviously, no one in 1909 contemplated the possibility that the automobile and airplane would one day carry far more travellers than the lordly railroad; both have been relegated to the corners of this print. How that regrettable eventuality came to pass is examined by Peter Lyon on the two preceding pages, and in more detail beginning on page 52.*

AMERICAN HERITAGE

The Magazine of History

SENIOR EDITOR
Bruce Catton

EDITOR
Oliver Jensen

MANAGING EDITOR
Robert Lincoln Reynolds

ART DIRECTOR
Murray Belsky

ART EDITOR
Joan Paterson Kerr

ARTICLES EDITOR
E. M. Halliday

ASSOCIATE EDITORS
Robert S. Gallagher   David G. Lowe
Barbara Klaw   John L. Phillips
Douglas Tunstell

COPY EDITOR
Brenda Niemand

EDITORIAL ASSISTANTS
Mary Dawn Earley   Rosemary L. Klein
Mary A. Hawkins   Joanne Shapiro

PUBLISHER
Darby Perry

ADVISORY BOARD
Allan Nevins, *Chairman*
Carl Carmer   Louis C. Jones
Gerald Carson   Alvin M. Josephy, Jr.
Marshall B. Davidson   Howard H. Peckham
John A. Garraty   Francis S. Ronalds
Eric F. Goldman   S. K. Stevens

AMERICAN HERITAGE is published every two months by American Heritage Publishing Co., Inc., 551 Fifth Avenue, New York, N.Y. 10017.

PRESIDENT
James Parton

CHAIRMAN, EDITORIAL COMMITTEE
Joseph J. Thorndike

MANAGING DIRECTOR, BOOK DIVISION
Richard M. Ketchum

SENIOR ART DIRECTOR
Irwin Glusker

Correspondence about subscriptions should be sent to: American Heritage Subscription Office, 383 West Center Street, Marion, Ohio 43302. Single copies: $4.25. Annual subscriptions: $16.50 in U.S. and Canada; $17.50 elsewhere. An annual Index of AMERICAN HERITAGE is published in February, priced at $1.00. AMERICAN HERITAGE will consider but assumes no responsibility for unsolicited materials. Title registered U.S. Patent Office. Second-class postage paid at New York, N.Y., and at additional mailing offices.

Sponsored by
American Association for State & Local History · Society of American Historians

CONTENTS *February, 1968 · Volume XIX, Number 2*

COVER: It is primarily as first Chief Justice of the United States that most of his countrymen remember John Jay, and here he is in the robes of that office, as painted by one of the foremost portraitists of the day. Yet before he ascended the Supreme Court bench, five months after George Washington assumed the Presidency, Jay had served his country in numerous capacities so important that he may be fairly ranked as a Founding Father. AMERICAN HERITAGE begins on the following page a three-part study of Jay and his world, drawn from the Jay Papers at Columbia University by an outstanding historian, Richard B. Morris. The Stuart portrait is on display at the National Gallery of Art, on loan from Mrs. Arthur Iselin. *Back Cover:* This "sentimental," published in 1850 by Sarony & Major in New York, is now owned by the Smithsonian Institution. An article on "Love and Marriage" as seen by Sarony & Major's chief competitor, Currier & Ives, begins on page 40.

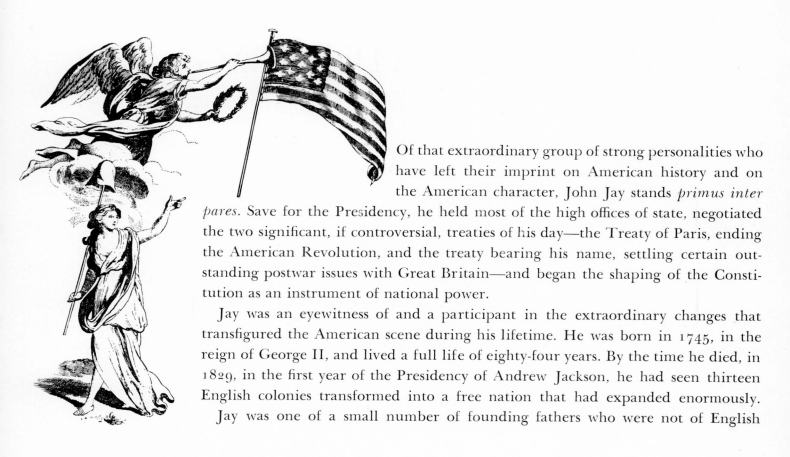

Of that extraordinary group of strong personalities who have left their imprint on American history and on the American character, John Jay stands *primus inter pares*. Save for the Presidency, he held most of the high offices of state, negotiated the two significant, if controversial, treaties of his day—the Treaty of Paris, ending the American Revolution, and the treaty bearing his name, settling certain outstanding postwar issues with Great Britain—and began the shaping of the Constitution as an instrument of national power.

Jay was an eyewitness of and a participant in the extraordinary changes that transfigured the American scene during his lifetime. He was born in 1745, in the reign of George II, and lived a full life of eighty-four years. By the time he died, in 1829, in the first year of the Presidency of Andrew Jackson, he had seen thirteen English colonies transformed into a free nation that had expanded enormously.

Jay was one of a small number of founding fathers who were not of English

THE WORLD

descent. His paternal grandfather was a Huguenot refugee from French religious persecution. His mother was of Dutch ancestry, a member of the land-rich Van Cortlandt family. Active in the practice of the law in New York City since shortly after his graduation from King's College (now Columbia University) in 1764, Jay withdrew from his profession on the eve of the Revolution and, despite some considerable doubts, threw himself into the patriot struggle for independence. He was the principal author of the New York constitution of 1777 and doubled as chief justice of his native state and one of its delegates to both Continental Congresses. In 1778 Congress elected Jay its president, a post which in form, if not substance, was the highest in the power of the Revolutionary government to confer. But these were only the beginnings of John Jay's service to his country. Ahead were a crucial wartime diplomatic mission to Spain, a key role in the writing of the Treaty of Paris and the *Federalist* papers, service as Secretary for Foreign Affairs under the

Confederation, and six useful years as the first Chief Justice of the United States.

Like other leading statesmen of his day, Jay carried on an extensive correspondence. He and his associates were amazingly articulate and refreshingly opinionated. He piled up and preserved a mountain of papers, which have never been published *in extenso;* the available editions of them cover only a fragment of the total and omit much of significance. This regrettable gap in the historical record is now being repaired. A few years ago Columbia University acquired many Jay documents from his descendants, and over the past half-dozen years it has been securing photocopies of all letters to or from Jay not in its collection. Archives on two continents have been ransacked in search of other relevant material. Columbia's Jay Collection now totals some twenty thousand items. Plans are well advanced to publish Jay's unpublished papers and a calendar of the entire collection.

From these papers three articles have been especially prepared and annotated for AMERICAN HERITAGE by their editor, the distinguished historian Richard B.

OF JOHN JAY

Morris, Gouverneur Morris Professor of History at Columbia and author of many outstanding books, the most recent being *The Peacemakers,* an account of the negotiation of the Treaty of Paris. The articles cover three distinct periods of Jay's life. The first, which begins on the following page, documents his adventures on his voyage to Spain in 1779 and the difficulties he faced in his diplomatic mission there. The second, which will appear in a forthcoming issue, illuminates Jay's observations and those of his correspondents on the course of the Confederation government during his years—1784 to 1789—as its Secretary for Foreign Affairs. The last article will highlight his views as a high Federalist politician, views formulated for the most part after he had left the Supreme Court bench, during his two terms as governor of New York and afterward during his long years of retirement at his country seat at Bedford, New York. Most of the letters, diary entries, and reports have never before been published.   —*The Editors*

John Jay arrived in Spain under great disadvantages: he was a militant Protestant, he spoke no Spanish, and he had come to beg money for an upstart republic rebelling against another monarchy. But he was a shrewd, stubborn negotiator.

THE JAY PAPERS I:

Edited and Annotated

John Jay was only thirty-three when Congress picked him for the delicate assignment to Madrid. A tall, spare figure with aristocratic bearing (left), he never forgot for a moment that he was a lawyer, and he had a lawyer's capacity for close analysis and a lawyer's caution both in action and language. Lacking neither self-assurance nor self-esteem, he had his own peculiar streak of obstinacy and was the kind of man who is not easily intimidated. These were some of the reasons behind his selection. But Congress also felt that court circles at Madrid would be impressed by Jay's rank among the patriots and believed that he would favor France's war aims and thereby prove a less obnoxious choice than some of the volubly anti-Gallican members of the isolationist wing of Congress.

France's good will was important. She had come into the war as an ally of America in early 1778. Spain had secretly agreed to intervene on France's side in the spring of 1779 and was openly at war with England a few months later. Sympathetic to one Bourbon house, Jay might be counted upon to persuade the frugal, devout, and highly intelligent Charles III (right), the hawk-visaged Bourbon ruler of Spain, of the merits of America's cause.

America had great expectations of Spain, including large-scale aid and even an alliance. She also assumed that Spain, once she was in the war, would be willing to allow Americans to ship goods down the Mississippi, which, as a result of a transfer of territory from France to Spain in 1763, was now Spain's exclusive preserve. There was little point in talking about a trans-Appalachian nation while navigation of the Mississippi was barred to its people. The furtherance of all these expectations, then, was John Jay's mission when he and his wife of five years, Sarah Van Brugh Livingston, stepped aboard the Continental frigate Confederacy *at Chester, Pennsylvania, on Delaware Bay on October 20, 1779.*

Sarah was the beautiful and gracious daughter of William Livingston, governor of New Jersey and a leading patriot intellectual. She worshipped her "Mr. Jay," senior to her by ten years, and he in turn was deeply in love with his "Sally." Their marriage proved a tender and affectionate, as well as a durable, partnership. The Jays left their three-and-a-half-year-old son Peter Augustus in the care of Sally's parents, but

MISSION TO SPAIN

RICHARD B. MORRIS

took in his place a twelve-year-old nephew, Peter Jay Munro. In addition, Jay, doubtless by persuasion of his wife, chose as his personal secretary Sally's ill-natured and somewhat overbearing brother, Colonel Henry Brockholst Livingston, a twenty-two-year-old veteran of the Revolutionary War. Also accompanying the Jays was William Carmichael of Maryland, whom Congress had designated as secretary to the Jay mission. Among their fellow passengers was Jay's friend Conrad Alexandre Gérard, the retiring French minister plenipotentiary to the United States, and Mme. Gérard.

Before departure, Sally received a touching farewell message from her father as well as a greeting from General Washington. To his boyhood friend and former law partner Robert R. Livingston (a second cousin of Sally's), soon to be Secretary for Foreign Affairs, John Jay sent a homemade private cipher.

His Most Catholic Majesty Charles III had curbed the Inquisition and launched economic reforms. But he had scant sympathy for rebels, and would not receive Jay at court. Goya painted him dressed for the hunt, his major passion.

Trenton, 7 October 1779

Dear Sally,

It is with great pain that I am obliged to part with you across a wide Ocean, and to a foreign Land. . . . may God Almighty keep you in his holy Protection, and if it should please him to take you out of this World, receive you into a better. And pray my dear Child, suffer not the Gaities and Amusements of the World, and the particular Avocations of what is called *high Life,* to banish from your Mind an habitual sense of an all-present Deity, or to interrupt you in paying him the homage you owe Him. With my most ardent Wishes for your good Voyage and safe Return I am
your affectionate Father
WIL. LIVINGSTON

West-point, October 7th, 1779

General Washington presents his most respectful compliments to Mrs. Jay. Honoured in her request by General St. Clair he takes pleasure in presenting the inclosed [a lock of Washington's hair], with thanks for so polite a testimony of her approbation and esteem. He wishes most fervently, that prosperous gales —and unruffled Sea—and every thing pleasing and desirable, may smooth the path she is about to walk in.

William Livingston

Henry Brockholst Livingston

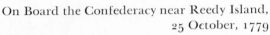

Sarah Livingston Jay

On Board the Confederacy near Reedy Island,
25 October, 1779

Dear Robert.

Accept my Thanks for your very friendly Letter. It recalled to my Mind many Circumstances on which it always dwells with Pleasure. I should have been happy in a personal Interview before my Departure, but since that has become impossible, let us endeavour to supply it by a regular and constant correspondence. To render this the more useful and satisfactory a Cypher will be necessary. There are twenty six Letters in our alphabet. Take twenty six Numbers in Lieu of them thus. [Jay then listed the letters of the alphabet and arbitrarily assigned a numerical equivalent to each. Thus, *a* was 5, *d* was 11, *h* was 10, etc.]

Remember in writing in this Way to place a , after each number, and a ; or : or a - after each Word. This will prevent Confusion. It will be unnecessary to write a whole Letter in Cypher. So many Words in Cypher as will blind the Sense will be sufficient, and more safe, as a Discovery will thereby be rendered more difficult. God bless you.

I am your affectionate Friend
JOHN JAY

The stormy voyage of the Confederacy *is depicted in the letters of Sally Jay to her mother, Susannah French Livingston. Jay himself appears to have been much too seasick to attend to formal correspondence. Sally's first letter is dated December 12.*

My dear mama,

. . . We embarked at Chester on the 20th of October, but did not lose sight of land 'till the 26th, when we launched out to sea with a brisk gale. The very first evening we were all seized with that most disagreeable sickness peculiar to our situation; my brother, Peter,

and myself soon recovered, but my dear Mr. Jay suffered exceedingly at least five weeks and was surprisingly reduced; I imagine his health would have been much sooner restored had not our passage been so very unpleasant.

About 4 o'Clock in the morning of the 7th of November, we were alarmed by an unusual noise upon deck, and what particularly surprised me, was the lamentations of persons in distress: I called upon the Captain to inform me the cause of this confusion that I imagined to prevail; but my brother desired me to remain perfectly composed, for that he had been upon deck but an half an hour before and left every thing in perfect security.

Perfect security! Vain words! don't you think so mamma? And so indeed they proved. For in that small space of time we had been deprived of nothing less than our bow-sprit, fore-mast, main-mast, and missenmast; so that we were in an awkward situation rendered still more so by a pretty high southeast wind and a very rough sea that prevailed then; however our misfortunes were only began, the injury received by our rudder, the next morning, served to compleat them. . . . let my benevolent mamma imagine the dangerous situation of more than 300 souls tossed about in the midst of the ocean, in a vessel dismasted

William Carmichael   *Conrad Alexandre Gérard*

William Livingston, Jay's father-in-law, was a patriot whom Tories called "the Don Quixote of the Jerseys." He represented New Jersey in both Continental Congresses and served as her governor for fourteen years. His son, Henry Brockholst Livingston, accompanied the Jays to Spain, where his arrogance and lack of discretion made him a trial. This portrait was made years later, when he was a distinguished justice of the United States Supreme Court. Sarah Livingston Jay, the Governor's daughter, was only twenty-three when she and her "Mr. Jay" took ship for Spain. Also aboard were William Carmichael, secretary of the mission, and M. Gérard, retiring as France's minister to America.

and under no command [*i.e.*, rudderless] at a season too that threatned approaching inclemency of weather. . . . I . . . assure you that in no period of our distress, though ever so alarming did I once repine, but incited by his [Jay's] amiable example, I gave fear to the winds and chearfully resigned myself to the dispensations of the Almighty.

Your whole family love Mr. Jay, but you are not acquainted with half his worth, nor indeed are any of his friends, for his modesty is equal to his merit. It is the property of a diamond (I've been told) to appear most brilliant in the dark; and surely a good man never shines to greater advantage than in the gloomy hour of adversity; in scenes of that kind I have lately beheld with pleasure, and even admiration, the firmness and serenity of mind that evidently shone out in the countenance of our invaluable friend. May he long, very long, be preserved a blessing to his connections and a *useful* as well as disinterested friend to his Country. . . . After our misfortunes on the 7th and 8th of November . . . a council of the officers was held to consider where it was most expedient to bend our course and it was unanimously concluded by them that it would be impossible to reach Europe at this season, with a ship in the condition that ours was. They were likewise united in opinion that the southern direction was the only one that offered a prospect of safety, and of the Islands, Martinico [Martinique] was the most eligible, for it's commodious harbour and the probability of being supplied with materials to refit: accordingly the first fair wind that offered (which was not 'till near three weeks from the above mentioned Aera) was embraced in pursuance of the advice given by the officers: and after having passed through very blustering, squally latitudes, we are now in smooth seas, having the advantage of trade-winds which blow directly for the Island; nor are we, if the calculations made are just, more than 220 miles distant from the destined port.

. . . [December 7] happened to be a merry [day] to the sailors . . . for crossing the tropick [*i.e.*, of Cancer] they insisted upon an antient custom of shaving and ducking every person that had not crossed it before excepting only those who paid their fine. I could not forbear smiling at Peter's fate, who had been diverting himself with observing the operation performed on many of them, 'till they exclaimed at the injustice of exempting him, and insisted upon his being tarred at least. . . . Peter, sobbing, declared that had not his new coat been spoilt, he would not have regretted so much the difficulty of getting rid of the tar. Apropos of Peter, his behaviour throughout this voyage has charmed me; I thought I could trace his grand-father's firmness in the equanimity of the child. May the resemblance be increased and perpetuated in every disposition and action of his life. . . .

Martinico, December 26th, 1779

Join with me, my dear mamma and sisters in grateful acknowledgements to that supreme Being whose indulgent care has preserved your friends through every danger, and permitted them to arrive in health in a most delightful Island, furnished with every thing necessary for health and almost every thing that can contribute to pleasure. On the 18th inst. early in the morning I was agreeably surprised to find that we were sailing [close] along the [most] verdant, romantic country I ever beheld. In that instant every disagreeable sensation arising from unpleasing circumstances during our voyage, gave place to the more mild and delightful emotions of gratitude.

At breakfast we were visited by some of the planters who live near the shore, and from them we learnt that Mr. [William] Bingham [of Philadelphia, agent for

CONTINUED ON PAGE 85
A PORTFOLIO OF ILLUSTRATIONS BEGINS OVERLEAF

THE JAYS IN SPAIN

A PORTFOLIO

The Jays and their party arrived at Cadiz (below) on February 22, 1780. No one welcomed them, for Jay was accorded no official status by the Spanish court. On March 20, having sent William Carmichael ahead to get the lay of the land, the Jays—along with Brockholst Livingston, nephew Peter Munro, and their servants—set out for Madrid, four hundred miles away. Sally, who was pregnant, found "the awkwardness and filth of every thing" beyond description, particularly the two mule-drawn carriages in which they travelled. "They have the impudence to call them coaches," she wrote to her sister; "it's true they are made of wood and have four wheels, but there the resemblance ceases." The coachmen overcharged them outrageously, and when they stopped for the night at an inn, the mules were quartered in an adjoining room and the bells around the animals' necks kept the Jays awake. For the most part the Americans found the Spanish countryside as bleak as Francisco Goya's painting Winter *(right) suggests. In Don Quixote's La Mancha, Sally wrote, they "looked but in vain for those large trees that sometimes afforded a safe retreat for the affrighted squire." Cordova had caught Sally's fancy, but the businesslike Jay cut short all her sight-seeing and pressed on to Madrid.*

ACROSS
THE COUNTRYSIDE
TO
MADRID

The Harvesters

Brawl in Front of an Inn

FIGHTING ON STILTS

ASH WEDNESDAY

The route to Madrid took the Jays through Andalusia, La Mancha, and Castile. By American standards the lot of the peasants, whose lives Francisco Goya was beginning to capture in paintings like these, was miserable. Nevertheless, they retained the dignity and joie de vivre *so evident in Goya's canvases. Their amusements (above) were simple. Their religious festivals (right) were of course incomprehensible to the staunchly Protestant Jays.*

As travellers, John and Sally were hardly simpatico: *they brought their own food, ate it with their own utensils, and carried their own folding beds, complete with "musketto" nets. Before settling down for the night in an inn, Sally would send in her maids to clear their rooms of "some half dozen filthy beds and several loads of dirt . . . fleas, lice, buggs etc." Her husband grumbled about the rates. "We all slept in our own Beds," he wrote. "They charged us for 14 Beds though our number including Servants amounted only to 8. . . . On observing this to them we were told that there were so many Beds in the Rooms in which we had slept . . . that we might have used them all if we pleased. We remarked that it was impossible for Eight persons to use fourteen Beds; they replied that was not their fault." But in the end Jay capitulated: "There was no Remedy and I paid it."*

AN
EMPIRE
AT
SUNSET

Madrid, which the Jays reached on April 4, 1780, was the capital of an empire already in decline. Under Charles III's son and grandson, in fact, Napoleon would conquer the entire Iberian Peninsula; soon, one by one, Spain's New World colonies would rise in revolt. When Jay arrived, however, the rumble of doom was inaudible, and king and grandee still lived extravagantly. At Aranjuez (above), one of five places where Charles held court, the elaborate equestrian display known as the Parejas Reales, *or "Royal Pairs," was still in fashion. Jay, partly because of his own democratic tastes, partly because of his lowly status at court, avoided such occasions. "This Pageantry may be proper in Monarchies," he wrote to a family friend, "and may entertain those who seldom entertain themselves." He preferred long solitary walks, meanwhile longing for the day "when the duties of a Citizen will permit me to return from this honorable Exile." He did, however, attend a* corrida *in Madrid's Plaza Mayor (right). "Mr. Jay and myself went yesterday to a Bull-fight," Brockholst Livingston wrote to his father, "which is the only diversion this town affords—and a cruel one it is ... Except the Gladiators I never read of anything more inhuman.... What surprised me most was the pleasure the Spanish Ladies received from the death of the poor animals —Indeed unless a great many horses are killed they call it a very poor feast."*

PLAZA DMADRID

DOUBLE DEALINGS AT MADRID

Don José de Gálvez

Father Thomas Hussey

While John Jay was en route to Madrid, backstairs negotiations were in progress there which, had Jay known of them, might have made him turn around and go home. Spain was at war with England, but she was now ready to come to terms. The intermediaries were a slippery Irish priest named Thomas Hussey and a social-climbing British playwright named Richard Cumberland. If England would agree to give up Gibraltar and the Floridas, Spain would make peace with her and refuse to recognize the independence of her thirteen rebellious colonies. Charles III's foreign minister, the Conde de Floridablanca (opposite page), was in fact never in sympathy with Jay's country; he wanted to see it a feudal dependency. These intrigues were still going on when Jay arrived. Moreover, he had got off on the wrong foot by making his initial approach not to Floridablanca but to José de Gálvez, the Minister of the Indies. That contretemps was soon smoothed over, but in Floridablanca, a shrewd provincial lawyer who had helped Charles III get the Jesuits expelled from Spain, John Jay faced a formidable adversary. For Jay, with all the cards stacked against him, a frustrating time lay ahead.

Richard Cumberland

Exͫo Sor Conde de Floridablanca.
Ministro que fué del Rey Carlos III.

PAINTING BY LUIS PARET; MUSEO DEL PRADO

THE KING IN SPLENDOR

Charles III, a widower, took luncheon alone. Churchmen and grandees stood and servants bowed the knee; only the King's hunting dogs might sit in the royal presence. This romantic painting contrasts strongly with Goya's realistic portrait on page 9. Poor Jay never saw either the myth or the reality: in two years at court he was never presented to the King.

The Great

By ALLAN

In November, 1919, and again in January, 1920, federal agents of the Department of Justice conducted a series of lightning-like raids on private houses and public buildings in cities across the United States and took into custody upwards of three thousand aliens suspected of plotting to overthrow the government. The mass arrests were enthusiastically acclaimed as Attorney General A. Mitchell Palmer's answer to "the sinister agitation of men and women aliens . . . either in the pay or under the criminal spell of Trotsky and Lenine." Indeed, within hours of the January roundup, William J. Flynn of the Bureau of Investigation (now the F.B.I.) told newsmen, "I believe that with these raids the backbone of the radical movement in America is broken."

If, as some have said, A. Mitchell Palmer was "a nervous man," he had a great deal of company in the spring and summer of 1919. Only a year later, William Allen White was to write a friend, "What a God-damned world this is! . . . If anyone had told me ten years ago that our country would be what it is today . . . I should have questioned his reason." It was a sentiment that many Americans had known in the months following World War I; for amidst the normal but unsettling confusions that marked the nation's transition from war to peace, there had appeared signs of deep-seated dislocations seemingly unlike any the country had experienced before.

There was, to begin with, considerable uncertainty over the peace treaty that Wilson had brought back from Versailles. As the Senate and the nation argued over its terms, a bitter debate on the League of Nations unleashed political passions lately held in check by a wartime truce. A business recession had set in, and although it was not unexpected, its crippling effects were intensified by a series of explosive industrial disputes.

Labor and management had been uneasy partners under federal controls during the war; now they were again familiar antagonists in what, by the year's end, totalled 3,600 separate strikes. Collective bargaining, higher wages, shorter work days, and union recognition were generally the issues at stake, but as violence and instability mounted—riots were common that year—the labor unrest took on a sinister cast. Inevitably there were those who remembered the old slogan of the discredited and now nearly defunct Industrial Workers of the World: "Every strike is a little revolution and a dress rehearsal for the big one." Typical headlines of the day proclaimed: "Red Peril Here" . . . "Reds Directing Strike" . . . "Test for Revolution." By autumn, the widely respected *Literary Digest* warned, "Outside of Russia, the storm center of Bolshevism is in the United States."

A Life *cartoon strikingly expressed the fears of many in 1919.*

In 1919 the U.S. Attorney General revolutionaries and deported them was a national hero; he dreamed

Red Scare

L. DAMON

A. Mitchell Palmer looked right for a tough Attorney General.

swooped down on alleged Bolshevik

by the boatload. For a while he

of the White House. But then . . .

There seemed to be, indeed, cause for alarm. Communism had triumphed in Russia and in Hungary; semi-anarchy reigned in postwar Germany; and there was political unrest in Poland, Italy, India, and China. The Third International had been organized in the spring of 1919 with world-wide revolution as its goal, and in the summer not one but two Communist parties were formed in the United States.

A far more frightening phenomenon had also appeared. On April 29, Mayor Ole Hanson of Seattle, Washington, had received a package containing sulphuric acid and dynamite caps. The triggering device had failed to operate, however, and Hanson, an outspoken foe of the I.W.W. and other radical groups, survived; he told reporters that the infernal machine was "big enough to blow out the side of the County-City Building."

Hardly had the papers carried that story when a brown-paper parcel, bearing the return address of Gimbel Brothers in New York, arrived at the Atlanta, Georgia, home of Senator Thomas W. Hardwick. The Senator, chairman of the Committee on Immigration, was not in, and a maid unwrapped the package. This time the detonator functioned properly and the parcel exploded, ripping off her hands.

By nightfall, the Hardwick bombing was front-page news. Charles Kaplan, a New York postal clerk on his way home by subway, was alerted by the newspaper description of the package delivered to the Senator's home. He quickly changed trains and hurried back to the General Post Office, where he remembered having seen sixteen small, brown-paper boxes set aside on a shelf because of insufficient postage. They were there, all with counterfeit Gimbel labels, and each addressed to a high-ranking government official or a well-known private citizen. Included were Attorney General Palmer, Secretary of Labor William B. Wilson, Supreme Court Justice Oliver Wendell Holmes, Jr., Judge Kenesaw Mountain Landis, John D. Rockefeller, and J. P. Morgan, Jr. Every package contained a bomb.

During the next week, watchful postal inspectors elsewhere in the country turned up sixteen more, each in its distinctive wrapper and addressed to a prominent person. The identity of the sender was never learned, but the newspapers and probably a majority of the public believed that the parcels had come from a Red bomb shop.

A month later, on June 1, seven explosions in five eastern cities ripped apart homes, public buildings, and a rectory, killing one man. In Washington that same night, an assassin came after the Attorney General again. Palmer had been reading in the first-floor library of his home in a quiet residential section of the city. At about eleven o'clock he put aside his book and went upstairs. He and Mrs. Palmer had just retired when the thump of something hitting the front porch echoed through the house and a violent explosion shattered windows throughout the neighborhood. The Palmers were unhurt, but the downstairs front of the house, including the library, was ruined. On the lawn, in the street, and on the sidewalk of Assistant Secretary of the Navy Franklin Delano Roosevelt's home opposite, "great chunks of human being" told the story. What had saved the Palmers from death was the clumsiness of the bomber, who evidently had stumbled and fallen, dropping the bomb before it could do serious damage to anyone but himself. Near the shattered body on Palmer's lawn and scattered along the street lay some fifty copies of *Plain Words,* an anarchist pamphlet that promised death to government officials ("There will have to be murder; we will kill. . . .") and proclaimed the triumph of the revolution.

Although, according to a reporter, Palmer remained "the coolest and most collected person" in the crowd that gathered to examine the wreckage, by morning he was understandably a badly frightened man. As he learned of the other bombings elsewhere on the eastern seaboard, he saw it all as part of a Red conspiracy to destroy the American way of life. He must act to save it.

The Attorney General had little difficulty persuading Congress to grant the Justice Department funds for the task. Yet as the summer of 1919 came on, Palmer appeared to be hesitating. The slowness of his preparations came as no surprise to his friends; he had always been a meticulous and somewhat cautious planner. But to many editors who daily ran stories of new Red plots, the Attorney General seemed reluctant to crush the threat the nation faced.

In truth, Palmer was at this point uncertain about the course he should follow. After the excitement of the bombings had died down, and despite the speed with which he had sought congressional aid, he became increasingly skeptical that the Reds were as active as many people claimed. Several of his close advisers predicted that the bombers would strike again and again; nothing of the kind happened. They warned that the Fourth of July would bring Bolshevik uprisings in major cities; the day passed quietly. Palmer adopted a policy of watchful waiting.

In part, his liberalism restrained him. A Wilsonian to the core, he believed strongly in the constitutional protections of the Bill of Rights, which as Attorney General he had sworn to uphold. He had been elected to Congress in 1908 with support from Pennsylvania steelworkers, coal miners, and clay-pit laborers, many of whom were recent immigrants. Now, years later, he continued to think of himself as "a radical friend of labor," and despite public pressures to the contrary, he had thus far refused to intervene in the strikes that were crippling the economy.

That kind of liberal restraint had marked his entire political career and, he was sure, had helped him move with comparative ease from the obscurity of a Pennsylvania law practice to the prominence of a Cabinet post. Given the right set of circumstances, it might conceivably carry him on to greater power and prestige in the White House itself.

Such a thought was not an idle dream, for at forty-seven the Attorney General was superbly equipped for the part. Tall, trim, and handsome, Palmer used his many talents with skill and grace. Besides his commanding physical presence, he had a quick and active mind, self-assurance in abundance, and above all, boundless energy. If—as one biographer has written—he was at times "too combative, too dogmatic, and too conceited" for his own good, he nevertheless had made more friends than enemies in high places. And if—as another has noted—his major weakness lay in his effort always "to win power by carefully attuning himself to what he felt were the strong desires of most Americans," he was no mere opportunist. He chose the issues he would support as much from deep personal belief as from political expediency.

Born of Quaker parents of moderate means, he was determined, he once wrote, "to be somebody," and his drive for power did not slacken as the years wore on. Graduating *summa cum laude* from Swarthmore before he was nineteen, he read law in the office of a former congressman, entered a lucrative practice at Stroudsburg, and soon became embroiled in the free-wheeling political life of the local scene. By 1909 he was in Washington, where he swiftly rose to a position of leadership. At the end of his first year in the House, he secured a seat on the powerful Ways and Means Committee, placed himself in the forefront of the progressive Democratic wing, and during three successive terms became identified with tariff reform and the cause of labor.

At the Baltimore convention of 1912 he delivered his state's delegation to Woodrow Wilson, hoping for the post of Attorney General as a reward. But the expected appointment fell through: instead, Wilson decided to name him Secretary of War. "I am a man of peace," Palmer said, declining the offer, and he returned to the House once more. Two years later he suffered his first major setback when, acceding to the President's blandishments, he entered a hopeless Senate race in Pennsylvania and went down to defeat.

With America's entry into World War I, Palmer was again in the national news. Despite his professed pacifism he was fiercely patriotic; "I made up my mind that I just must get into it somehow, even if I had to carry a gun as a private," he told a friend. His change of heart, however, never carried him to that extreme, and he accepted Wilson's appointment as custodian of property in the United States owned by enemy aliens. For over a year he worked with such vigor and aggressiveness that the press labelled him the "Fighting Quaker," a title he wore as a badge of honor. Some of his critics suspected that his prowar views were tied to his political hopes, but Palmer emerged from the war with his popularity intact.

The raids of 1919–20 launched one of Palmer's young assistants, J. Edgar Hoover, on a lifelong crusade against left-wingers.

In March, 1919, he claimed his long-awaited reward, appointment as Attorney General of the United States.

He had been three months on the job when the bomb burst outside his home. Despite his uncertainty about the seriousness of the Red threat, Palmer did proceed to reorganize the Department of Justice to cope with the problem. By August he had created the General Intelligence Division, a special arm within the Bureau of Investigation, to root out the Communist conspiracy if one existed. He gave charge of the new bureau to J. Edgar Hoover, a twenty-four-year-old lawyer who, in the summer of 1917, had come fresh from George Washington University Law School to serve in the Department of Justice as an aide in charge of Enemy Alien Registration. Now, as a special assistant to Palmer, Hoover with his G.I.D. put together an elaborate filing system of over 200,000

cross-indexed cards containing information on 60,000 persons, several hundred newspapers, and dozens of organizations considered dangerous to the national interest.

But this quiet, systematic preparation did nothing to allay the fears of the public, or to satisfy their panicky desire for drastic action. For if the nation had been alarmed by the riots and bombs of the spring, it was terrified by the events of late summer and early fall.

July brought race riots in Cleveland and in Washington, D.C. Labor unrest continued without letup all summer long. Then, during the first week of September, the Communist party and the Communist Labor party emerged from separate Chicago conventions. Almost immediately there were reports that their combined memberships exceeded 100,000; some accounts placed the number at six times that figure. Recent studies have shown that the most modest of these estimates was greatly exaggerated; but in the fall of 1919 it was the rumors that counted.

Already groups like the National Security League had published stories to the effect that most labor unions, the leading universities, some churches, the League of Women Voters, and a host of other organizations were under Red control or sympathetic to the cause. Some newspapers asserted that outspoken reformers like John Dewey, Roscoe Pound, Jane Addams, Robert M. La Follette, and Thorstein Veblen were linked to the growing Red menace.

In such an atmosphere and at such a time, it was difficult to know what was true and what was not. But as Bolshevism in Russia hardened into tyranny, and as magazine articles by the score rang continuous changes on the same terrifying theme of *it must not happen here,* even those who had discounted the earlier scare headlines became alarmed.

In September the Boston police went on strike. Two days of limited violence and looting followed before volunteers and some 5,000 National Guardsmen restored order. Governor Calvin Coolidge, who had done little to correct the situation, then sent his famous telegram to the A.F. of L.'s Samuel Gompers saying, "There is no right to strike against the public safety by anybody, anywhere, any time" (see "The Strike That Made a President" in the October, 1963, AMERICAN HERITAGE). Later in the month federal troops were sent to quiet the nation's steel towns, where a bitter dispute had just begun. When 394,000 coal miners left the pits on November 1, the public feared the beginning of a nationwide general strike, or worse.

Meanwhile, Attorney General Palmer had been suffering under a terrific barrage of public criticism. "I was shouted at from every editorial sanctum in

America from sea to sea," he complained later. "I was preached upon from every pulpit; I was urged to do something and do it now, and do it quick and do it in a way that would bring results." In mid-October of 1919, the Senate took up the cry; it unanimously demanded an explanation for Palmer's inaction, and in a censure resolution implied that he might well face removal from his post.

The Senate's censure was a harsh blow, especially in the light of Palmer's presidential dreams. Woodrow Wilson's debilitating stroke in mid-autumn had already awakened speculation among many men about possible successors in the election year ahead. How seriously Palmer took his own candidacy at this point is anybody's guess (he did not mention it openly until February, 1920); but he was too experienced a politician not to know that once he lost the public's favor he would be hard pressed to regain it. It is not surprising that a man of his ambition began to react profoundly to the clamor that he "do something."

Moreover, Palmer was surrounded by men who had long since become convinced that the Red menace was real. Among his Cabinet colleagues, Secretary of War Newton D. Baker, Secretary of the Navy Josephus Daniels, and Secretary of State Robert Lansing had been writing and speaking about the threat of revolution from early summer on. Even President Wilson had inserted antiradical themes in his speeches on behalf of the League a few days before he fell ill. But it was the men whom Palmer numbered among his closest advisers in the Department of Justice itself whose influence was greatest. They had taken the Reds very seriously from the start. To be sure, almost all the information they possessed had come from theoretical discussions in radical newspapers and books; there was little worthwhile evidence of active preparation for revolt. Nonetheless, to these advisers, where there was smoke there was probably fire. They were ready to act.

By November, Palmer was ready too. Now convinced by his own reading of anarchist literature that the nation was besieged by "thousands of aliens, who were the direct allies of Trotsky," he declared that the time had passed when it was possible or even desirable to draw "nice distinctions . . . between the theoretical ideals of the radicals and their actual violations of our national law."

The time for watching and waiting was over. "Like a prairie-fire," he himself wrote in *Forum* magazine the next year, "the blaze of revolution was sweeping over every institution of law and order. . . . It was eating its way into the homes of the American workman, its sharp tongues of revolutionary heat were licking the altars of the churches, leaping into the belfry of the school bell, crawling into the sacred corners of American homes, seeking to replace marriage vows with libertine law, burning up the foundations of society." To put out the fires, Palmer decided to enforce a part of the immigration code, introduced during the war, that outlawed anarchism in all its forms. Aliens who violated that code, even if only by reading or receiving anarchist publications, could be arrested and, if found guilty, deported.

There was a beautiful simplicity to Palmer's solution. Deportation hearings were neither lengthy nor complex. They were handled as executive functions by the immigration officers of the Department of Labor. Although the aliens were supposed to be protected by the procedural safeguards of the Bill of Rights, only minimum proof (usually a warrant of cause) was needed to show that some part of the immigration code had been violated. The rulings of

A few of the thousands of "Red" aliens rounded up by Palmer's men await a ferry to Boston's bleak Deer Island prison.

the hearing officers were, in effect, arbitrary, checked only by the construction of the deportation statutes, a possible appeal to the Secretary of Labor, or, in rare instances, by a writ of habeas corpus, which led to a federal court trial. Palmer decided to test both the effectiveness of deportation as an anti-Red measure, and the public's response.

On the night of November 7, 1919, federal agents from the Bureau of Investigation and city policemen quietly surrounded the Russian People's House on East Fifteenth Street in New York. Inside the four-story brownstone that served as a meeting place and recreation center for Russian aliens, some two hundred men and boys were at work in night-school classes. That evening was the anniversary of the Bolshevik uprising in Petrograd two years before, but the directors of the school had planned no special observance, even though the school's sponsor, the Federation of Unions of Russian Workers in the United States and Canada, had been a leading publisher of anarchist tracts.

Shortly after nine o'clock the agents swarmed into the building. "The harsh command to 'shut up, there, you,' brought silence" in the classrooms, the *New York Times* reported next day, and in the hush that followed, the agents announced that all present were under arrest. A teacher who asked why (for no warrants had been produced) took a blow in the face that shattered his glasses. Then, while some agents searched the bewildered suspects for weapons, city policemen tore open locked files, overturned desks, pulled down pictures from the wall, and rolled up rugs in an unsuccessful hunt for incriminating evidence. At last, no weapons having been found, they herded the prisoners toward the stairs and—as an investigator from the National Council of Churches reported later—forced them to run a gantlet of officers who lined the stairwell armed with blackjacks. By the time the suspects reached the agents' headquarters, thirty-three of them required medical treatment. Their bandaged heads and blackened eyes, the *Times* remarked, were "souvenirs of the new attitude of aggressiveness which had been assumed by the Federal agents against Reds or suspected Reds."

Elsewhere in the nation that night, federal officers in nine other cities east of the Mississippi raided other Russian centers. In all, about four hundred and fifty persons were rounded up. Before the night was over, more than half of them were released as innocent, but Attorney General Palmer was distinctly pleased with the results.

For by morning he was a national hero, praised by the very press that only the week before had been railing at him and demanding his resignation. Now, as one paper put it, he was "a tower of strength to his countrymen." His new answer to the Reds, said another, was "S.O.S.—Ship or Shoot." Still another suggested that the new year might bring a three-point trade program of "import—export—deport."

By December, Palmer was riding the crest of enthusiastic public support. Working quickly now, he secured deportation orders for 199 Russians who had been found guilty under the immigration law. Taken to Ellis Island, they were joined by fifty other deportees, including Alexander Berkman, the would-be assassin of Henry Clay Frick in the Homestead Strike twenty-seven years before, and Emma Goldman, a well-known anarchist writer whose work had allegedly inspired Leon Czolgosz to murder President McKinley. All 249 aliens were to be deported to Russia by way of Finland, the Finnish government having agreed to act in this case as the agent for the United States, which had yet to recognize the Bolshevik regime.

Although immigration officials had promised that no married men would be deported and that ample time would be given the aliens to settle their affairs, neither pledge was honored. In the early hours of December 21, the aliens boarded the *Buford,* an ancient army transport now nicknamed "the Soviet Ark." Two hundred fifty armed soldiers patrolled the decks, but, with the exception of a short-lived hunger strike, the voyage passed uneventfully. In mid-January, 1920, the *Buford* docked at Hango, Finland, and under a flag of truce—the Finns were now at war with Russia—the deportees passed into Soviet hands.*

Meanwhile Palmer readied a second attack on the Reds. If the November raid had netted hundreds, the new series would bring in thousands. Hoping to speed the process, Palmer asked Secretary of Labor Wilson to change that part of the deportation rules that permitted the aliens to secure counsel, and at the same time he requested a blanket deportation warrant to cover any aliens who might be arrested once the raids began. Wilson refused both requests, emphasizing that the immigrants, despite their lack of citizenship, were nonetheless entitled to the protection of the Bill of Rights. Palmer, no longer sounding like a confirmed liberal, insisted that all too often it was lawbreakers, not the innocent, who were protected by these legal safeguards, but Wilson held firm.

For the moment, the Attorney General was stymied. Then, in mid-December, Secretary Wilson went on sick leave. His duties were divided between Louis F. Post, his assistant, and John W. Abercrombie, the Labor Department's solicitor and a Palmer appointee. To Palmer's relief, Post, whom the press had labelled

CONTINUED ON PAGE 75

* After the furor attending their departure from the United States and the news of their arrival in Russia, the *Buford* deportees dropped out of sight. The majority apparently remained in Russia, but two, at least, did not. Berkman, ever the anarchist, was quickly disillusioned by what he found in the Communist state, and by 1925 had published two highly critical books, *The Bolshevik Myth* and *The Anti-climax*. He had, of course, left Russia by then, and he spent the remaining years of his life wandering aimlessly through Europe. He committed suicide in Nice, France, in 1936.

Following disagreements and an open break with the Bolsheviks in 1921, Emma Goldman too left the country and two years later wrote *My Disillusionment in Russia*. In 1924 she was permitted to re-enter the United States for a lecture tour under the terms of a curious arrangement whereby she was not permitted to discuss politics in public. She was not allowed to remain, however, and crossed the border into Canada. She died in Toronto in 1940.

On the late afternoon tide of August 13, 1850, over one hundred men and 160 tons of equipment sailed from New York Harbor for Matagorda Bay on the Texas coast. The party's goal was to draw a border of two thousand miles between the United States and its recently conquered neighbor to the south. The task would be long and arduous, for the line would run through what the survey commissioner came to call the "thorny and angular" landscapes of southern New Mexico and northern Sonora and Chihuahua—hot, barren stretches, rocky, saguaro-studded slopes, and piñon-pocked mesas. The new limits of national sovereignty would be delineated by instruments carted and jostled over thousands of rough, wearying miles.

The Treaty of Guadalupe Hidalgo, which had ended the Mexican War early in 1848, directed that the two governments each appoint a commissioner and a surveyor whose conclusions would be binding—as if inserted in the treaty before ratification. The United States had already appointed three chief commissioners: the first had died, the second had been discredited, and the third had resigned before taking up the work.

The latest commissioner, who assumed his duties less than two months before sailing, was John Russell Bartlett. Neither politician nor frontiersman, Bartlett was a scientist and artist, a thin, vigorous New York bookseller who was intimate with the likes of Albert Gallatin, John L. Stephens, and Edgar Allan Poe. Like Gallatin and Stephens, Bartlett's dedication to the cause of science was enhanced by a marked ability to communicate his ideas—in Bartlett's case, by word and brush.

Bartlett was a man of parts. Much of his early life was spent in Kingston, Canada, where he became adept with rod and rifle, and where he developed a more than nodding acquaintance with the wilderness. Later, as a young man back in his native Providence, Rhode Island, he devoted his leisure hours to painting and to such interests as geographical research, antiquities, philology, and ethnology. He pursued science and art simultaneously and was grateful to the influential friends who helped him to land the commissionership that would enable him to indulge both passions.

The overland journey from Matagorda Bay to El Paso, where the party would rendezvous with the Mex-

This portrait of John Bartlett was done in El Paso by Henry C. Pratt, the boundary commission's chief artist.

In 1850 John Russell Bartlett set out to draw up—and draw—a border between the United States and Mexico. He put up with an infernal wilderness, fractious colleagues, and a damsel ungrateful for his chivalry, but he left a rich legacy of art

An Artist Draws the Line

By ROBERT V. HINE

ican commission, was completed by mid-November. Bartlett's first group of Western drawings, made en route, showed a progression from leisurely Sunday painting to rapid lap-sketching. The transition was a response to the hardships of that first leg: the country had begun to show its teeth; there had been some rather ugly incidents of dissension, and some men had resigned. John Bartlett, Yankee bookseller, amateur scientist, and United States commissioner, was meeting the frontier Southwest. Nevertheless, he remained the model of urban culture, carrying toothbrush, teapot, and Seidlitz powders wherever he went, and travelling in a rockaway coach that also served as fortress and sleeping quarters.

The boundary commission spent a winter of delay and frustration in El Paso. Andrew B. Gray, the chief surveyor, was ill in Washington. Bartlett did not get on well with Robert McClellan, his chief astronomer-topographer, and demanded and received his resignation. But Bartlett decided to make at least a start, by establishing the "initial point" of westward departure for the boundary. He and the Mexicans under General García Conde agreed on a point on the Rio Grande

near Doña Ana, about forty miles north of El Paso. That arrangement—which would determine the latitude along which the boundary would be fixed—would come back to plague Bartlett, but for the time being, at least, work could begin.

In the spring of 1851 the expedition set up field headquarters at Santa Rita, an abandoned copper-mining settlement northwest of El Paso and a few miles east of the Continental Divide. It was an ideally located base camp, being just north of the specified latitude and within reasonable distance of the Gila River, the boundary's natural route farther west. Bartlett had hopes of finishing the survey all the way along the Gila to the junction of the Colorado River and being back in El Paso by the following winter.

The midsummer arrival of his key personnel did little to advance Bartlett's expectations. Surveyor Gray felt that the Bartlett-García Conde line should have been drawn only eight miles north of El Paso. A Texan, he saw Bartlett as a Yankee trying to rob the South of an easy route through the mountains for a transcontinental railroad. The new principal astronomer and chief of the scientific corps, James Graham,

TEXT CONTINUED ON PAGE 102
ILLUSTRATIONS CONTINUE OVERLEAF

The commission's trip from the Gulf coast to El Paso gave an indication of extremes to come. In September the thermometer hovered over 100°, but in early November the party had to wait out a snowstorm, sketched above by Bartlett.

This drawing of the rugged Guadalupe Pass, made on the return from one of the foraging trips into Mexico, was the basis of a lithograph that appeared in Bartlett's Narrative.

The survey jumped off from Santa Rita, an abandoned mining town near El Paso. This view of the base camp is by Seth Eastman (no kin to the Eastman who drew for Bartlett in California), who converted many survey sketches to water color.

Fording a stream. Pack mules sink in a quicksand

One of Bartlett's supply treks south was graced by the presence of a fifteen-year-old girl, Inez Gonzales, whose story, he felt, provided "full recompense for the trials and hardships attending our sojourn in this inhospitable wilderness." Inez, "artless, and interesting in appearance," had been captured near her native Santa Cruz by Indians, who sold her to Mexican traders. When the Mexicans came to the Santa Rita area planning a profitable resale, Bartlett heard of the scheme. Recalling that the Treaty of Guadalupe Hidalgo enjoined the United States to repatriate any Mexican captives, he sent some soldiers to free her. Bartlett now felt responsible for returning the "fair captive" to Santa Cruz, and Inez is shown above during a pause in the trip—some mules having bogged down in quicksand. Bartlett was warmed by the joyous reception Inez's family gave her but was shocked some months later, in July of 1852, to find the girl living with the captain of the garrison at Tubac, in Sonora. Bartlett regarded the captain as her "captor" and again offered her his protection, although she seemed to be content where she was. But Bartlett made his moral position quite clear, and perhaps effectively, for Inez and the captain were finally married, legitimizing the two sons she bore him.

Harrison Eastman did this fine water color from Bartlett's field sketch of part of the boundary to the south of Santa Rita.

In the fall of 1851 Bartlett was felled by typhoid and had to spend two and a half months at Ures, in southern Sonora. He complained at the lack of a fireplace, but otherwise life was pleasant, all things considered. There was an American doctor (a twenty-year resident of the area) to care for him, and he busied himself by studying the local agriculture and the languages of regional Indians. He read David Copperfield and Bancroft's History of the United States from his travelling library. In his Narrative, Bartlett mentions "a solitary date-tree within the limits of the town; but I could hear of no others near, and presume this . . . an exotic." It dominates the sketch at left.

The delicate pencil and wash drawing above, of a Chin-oh village near Monroeville, California, was done by Henry Brown.

The party refitted in California early in 1852. Henry Box Brown and Harrison Eastman were retained in San Francisco to supplement Bartlett's artistic efforts. (Brown was asked to accompany the survey to El Paso, but funds were too low to offer him an attractive fee.) From the Sacramento Valley, Brown wrote that he had been particularly taken with a group of Indians called the Chin-ohs. "They are very fine looking men with regular faces. I procured . . . an interior of a large council house 39 feet in diameter and twelve high into which I shall put a group gambling from studies taken on the spot, a singular & striking scene with a Rembrandt effect of chiar'oscuro." The result is seen at right.

The party resumed its eastward survey at Fort Yuma, where Pratt painted the confluence of the Colorado and the Gila.

Bartlett's sketch seems to belie his remark that "half the buildings of Tucson are tenantless and falling into ruin."

34

The journey from San Diego to Fort Yuma in the late spring of 1852 was one of the most trying the commission endured. The party often travelled at night to escape the insufferable heat; what wind there was brought no relief— Bartlett likened it to "the African sirocco . . . as though issuing from a heated furnace." At the fort, the commissioner's scientific curiosity began to reassert itself, and soon he was hurrying on, drawing with deep interest the giant saguaros near Tucson (lower left), and supervising the careful measurements of walls and foundations at ancient ruins like those of Casas Grandes in Chihuahua, seen at right in a sketch by Henry Pratt. As they moved east toward the Rio Grande, Bartlett and his group met several wagon trains of mid-westerners headed for California, and had to put up with the inevitable "Halloa, you're going the wrong way." The inhospitality of the wilderness was infinitely varied, even to a soaking rainstorm (below, in Seth Eastman's rendering) and flash flood on the Mexican plateau in August, just before Bartlett's return to El Paso.

On August 21, 1897, Joseph Pulitzer's New York *World* published an item that, for the astute reader, pertained not to one war but to two. The article ostensibly concerned the fate of a prisoner of war in Cuba, but it was also printed to escalate the intensity of quite another conflict—in New York. Headlined GENERAL WEYLER TO THE WORLD, it read, in part, "In a Personal Cable Message to *The World,* the Captain-General of Cuba Says that Evangelina Cisneros, the Beautiful Cuban Girl, Has Not Been Condemned or Even Tried as Yet." The newspaper went on to quote the cable, which was datelined Havana, August 20: "For judicial reasons there is on trial in the preliminary stages a person named Evangelina Cosio y Cisneros, who, deceitfully luring to her house the military commander of the Isle of Pines, had men posted secretly, who . . . attempted to assassinate him. This case is in the preliminary stages and has not as yet been tried by a competent tribunal, and consequently no sentence has been passed nor approved by me.

"I answer the *World* with the frankness and truth that characterizes all my acts. WEYLER."

The story of Evangelina Cosio y Cisneros, whom some called the most beautiful girl on the island of Cuba, comprised such a curious mixture of romance, intrigue, mystery, and controversy that it was to attract, in New York City, more fervent attention than the military and political events of the entire Cuban revolution.

The revolution itself had started in February of 1895, when a brilliant Cuban writer, poet, and orator, José Julian Martí, rallied his Cuban Revolutionary party to overthrow Spanish rule on the island. Although Martí was killed in the early fighting, the rebel cause was vigorously prosecuted by General Máximo Gómez y Báez and his poorly equipped and widely scattered army of about 30,000. By the summer of 1897, when the name of Evangelina Cisneros first began appearing in American newspapers, the revolutionary cause had not advanced appreciably. The fortunes of Evangelina and her family were at the lowest possible ebb. Her father, one of the rebel leaders, had been imprisoned two years before; she and her sister, dangerous persons in the eyes of the Spanish authorities, had already spent the better part of a year in confinement of one sort or another.

Evangelina Cisneros might have been as anonymous as the thousands upon thousands of other Cubans who languished in prisons and concentration camps during those revolutionary years from 1895 until 1898, had it not been for the other war more than 1,300 miles away. This was the battle of the press, waged by New York newspapers with a viciousness never before seen in the publishing world.

The two principal opponents were the New York *World* and the New York *Morning Journal* (later the

THE PERILS OF EVANGELINA

Being the thrilling account of the capture, imprisonment, and rescue of one of history's loveliest P.O.W.'s, and of how her plight kept the New York presses—and their editors—humming

By WILBUR CROSS

New York *Journal*). Pulitzer's *World* had been stampeding into prominence and was considered almost unbeatable from a circulation standpoint when, in November of 1895, William Randolph Hearst acquired the *Journal*. Although a great admirer of the *World,* Hearst had devoted several years to studying what Frank Luther Mott called "the formula for the successful sensational newspaper"; he was convinced he could put together a winning combination of talent to overcome all rivals. After all, he had already made a spectacular success of the San Francisco *Examiner,* which his father had bought and turned over to him.

One of the factors in the Hearst formula for the "new journalism" was to hire the best talent available. With the acquisition of the *Journal,* he immediately signed on some of the most brilliant newspapermen of the day, including Samuel S. Chamberlain as managing editor, noted cartoonist Homer Davenport, ace reporter Arthur McEwen, Stephen Crane, and Winifred Black, a famous "sob sister."

This Puck *cartoon of June, 1896, was prophetic, for the very next year there was indeed a center-stage melodrama featuring a bewhiskered Spanish villain, a resourceful American, and a beautiful Cuban maiden in distress.*

An even more important ingredient for success, however, was the development of sensational feature material that lured readers to the front page like flies to syrup. "Yellow journalism" was evolving: it was considered sound practice to exploit the ghastliest events imaginable in order to build circulation. Typical stories that were blown up out of all proportion to their news significance included the pathetic account of a child who bit into a stick of dynamite, thinking it was candy, to meet "an awful death"; the

description of a "maniac" engineer who went mad while operating a passenger-train locomotive; and the clinical tale of a girl running down the street with her "head all ablaze." Murder, rape, arson, suicide—violence of all sorts—were characteristic front-page fodder.

As the two newspapers maneuvered closer and closer to a pitched battle for circulation, the formula for success became somewhat modified. The isolated tale of brutality or sex was no longer sufficient. Editors began plotting ways of developing *continuing* stories as vehicles to accumulate and maintain larger readerships. Into this curious pattern of yellow journalism the name and misfortunes of Evangelina Cosio y Cisneros were to fit with resounding and unexpected impact.

When the *World* published the cable from General Weyler (Valeriano Weyler y Nicolau), the Spanish commander charged with the task of putting down the rebellion in Cuba, Evangelina's name was not entirely new to the front pages. Four days earlier, the *Journal* had told a melodramatic tale about a rebel leader's beautiful young daughter who, though only eighteen, was being held prisoner by the Spaniards and exposed to the lascivious eye of one of her captors. The story had many ingredients that fit the circulation-building formula—if some means could be found for running it in installments and developing a series of actions that would sustain reader interest while building to some sort of climax.

The *Journal* had introduced the story with a theme of "injustice"—the account of the innocent victim of Spanish misrule and cruelty. From the beginning, American sympathy had been with the rebels, the underdogs fighting (as America herself had once done) to win liberty from a Great Oppressor. Evangelina, therefore, symbolized all the little people, the patriots, who were being crushed underfoot. The *World,* rising to the challenge, took the stand that its rival was indulging in pure fiction—that Evangelina was not being oppressed in any way. It was for this reason that it published General Weyler's denial that there was any lack of justice in the Cisneros case.

The journalistic climate in which subsequent events developed can probably best be explained through an anecdote about William Randolph Hearst and the

Journal. By early 1897, Hearst had sent a number of journalists to cover the Cuban revolution, among them the famous correspondent Richard Harding Davis and the noted illustrator Frederic Remington. It is said that Remington quickly became bored and cabled Hearst: "EVERYTHING IS QUIET. THERE IS NO TROUBLE HERE. THERE WILL BE NO WAR. WISH TO RETURN." Hearst replied: "PLEASE REMAIN. YOU FURNISH THE PICTURES AND I'LL FURNISH THE WAR." The story illustrates an important rationale of the journalism of the 1890's: if a story isn't good enough, embellish it. In this kind of reportorial atmosphere, it was not surprising that the *Journal's* staff found great appeal and attraction in the Cisneros affair—a beautiful girl, mystery, a tropical setting, and the endangerment of feminine virtue.

By mid-August of 1897 a number of events had already occurred that made the story a natural. The whole thing had begun with an act of betrayal. On the night of June 21, 1895, Evangelina had been lying in bed in the darkness of her family's small farmhouse, when she was startled by a tapping on the door. She was expecting the return of her father, who had left that night with a small patrol to harass the Spanish forces. Instead, she found a neighbor, who told her that her father had been captured.

"But *how?*" asked Evangelina, incredulous that a man with her father's knowledge of the local terrain could have fallen into enemy hands. "Is he wounded?"

"No," came the pained reply. "He was captured without a struggle. One of his squad is a traitor. The patrol walked straight into an ambush."

Another ingredient that made the story appealing was the determination of the young girl in her prolonged efforts to save her father from the death sentence or from imprisonment so harsh that it would result in his death. Every morning she walked to the prison, Cienfuegos, to beg for an appointment with General Martínez de Campos, the commanding officer. Her efforts were futile until one day she learned the tragic news that her father was to be executed. She fainted immediately, slumping to the pavement just outside the prison enclosure. By chance a young Spanish lieutenant saw her and ordered his men to place her in the shade. Naturally, since she was not at all unat-

tractive, the Spaniard saw to it that his unexpected charge was properly revived.

"What are you doing here?" he asked Evangelina when she had regained consciousness. He listened with growing sympathy as she told how her father, "a brave patriot, simply doing what he felt was his duty," had been thrown into prison and condemned to death, and how she had futilely attempted to get an audience with General de Campos to plead for mercy. The lieutenant, easily won by her large dark eyes and patrician manner, readily agreed to help her. (It so

Above, Evangelina poses in the dress she wore as she escaped from her cell (upper right). In the other drawing, a Recojidas inmate receives rations.

happened that he was the General's son, which made it somewhat easier for him to make a plea for leniency.) He was only partly successful, however; the General agreed only to commute the death sentence to imprisonment in Ceuta, a penal colony in Africa.

"My father would never survive the fevers and heat," said Evangelina.

"Then your only hope," replied the General, "is to plead with Captain-General Valeriano Weyler."

Naïvely, Evangelina made her way to Havana to talk to Weyler, nicknamed the Butcher for his harshness in dealing with rebel sympathizers. Predictably, the tough old soldier at first rejected any pleas for clemency, although he was enough of a Spanish gentleman to grant an immediate audience to the dark-eyed beauty. Finally he was swayed by Evangelina's display of self-sacrifice. "If you will send my father to the penal colony on the Isle of Pines, instead of to Ceuta," she said, "my sister Carmen and I will accompany him as political prisoners. In that way, you will be assured that he cannot become involved in further rebellion." The Butcher granted her request.

LEFT: CULVER PICTURES; ALL OTHERS: *The Story of Evangelina Cisneros, Told by Herself,* 1897

The señorita scrubs a prison floor in the sketch at top; below, in her get-away getup, she is seen with Karl Decker, who freed her from Weyler (right).

Banishment to the small island off Cuba's southwest shore apparently was not as grim as sympathetic Americans made it out to be. One source even described life as "a moderately pleasant existence" during the months in 1896 when Cisneros and his two daughters lived there. They occupied one section of a red-tiled adobe building that had been divided into six sets of living quarters, with a large communal patio. Rather than existing in virtual "slavery," as some newspapers later suggested, the prisoners seem to have been assigned relatively light duties, with

adequate food, clothing, and other supplies. In fact, Evangelina Cisneros would have gone unnoticed in the American press had it not been for a routine change of command on the Isle of Pines.

In July of 1896, the commander of the island's penal colony was transferred and replaced by Colonel José Berriz, a short, dark man with coal-black hair and whiskers, and green eyes—some considered him handsome. One reason he received the assignment was that the island was considered a plush post, a suitable command for a man who was a favorite of Weyler's and a nephew of Spanish Premier Marcelo de Azcarraga.

Life for the prisoners now began to change. Berriz wanted to emulate Weyler and thus imposed harsh restrictions on the rebels under his charge. At the same time, he began to look on Evangelina with considerable warmth. Unfortunately for all concerned, it was not reciprocal. Not only was she repulsed by this little, bewhiskered man, but she was romantically involved with another prisoner, Emilio Betancourt, a handsome young Cuban who had been courting her for some months.

Late one night, Colonel Berriz quietly went to Evangelina's room. The circumstances of this clandestine visit have never been clearly established, although the incident was repeatedly used by both pro- and anti-Cuban interests to generate propaganda. The Spanish version of the matter is that Evangelina encouraged the Colonel's advances and lured him to her quarters, where other prisoners were waiting to assassinate him. The rebels maintained that Evangelina's only enticement was her own natural beauty, which she could hardly conceal. No matter which story is true, it seems clear that Colonel Berriz had threatened to punish her father severely for minor infractions, and the rebel assumption was that he intended to take advantage of Evangelina's filial loyalty by promising to be lenient if the girl would become his mistress.

Whether by prearrangement or not, Evangelina screamed as the Colonel approached. The screams brought a number of other prisoners who, in the darkness, seized the Colonel and threw him to the floor. Then, in a sudden panic, the prisoners scattered, knowing there would be immediate reprisals. Berriz yelled for the guard, bellowed accusations of "assassi-

CONTINUED ON PAGE 104

THE LOVE LETTER.

Love & Marriage

Though some today might be inclined to call it Love and Mirage, Currier & Ives' idealized view of the tender process was the popular one in the days when all suitors were expected to see the importance of being earnest, and when all chased young ladies were, of course, chaste

THE DECLARATION.

Mid-nineteenth-century America was, as Russel Crouse put it in Mr. Currier and Mr. Ives, *a world "almost complex in its simplicity." The two printmakers, he wrote, dealt only with "emotions that were on the surface"—and that certainly is true in this wooing and wedding series, whose captions tell us far more than the principals' expressions. But this was an age of sentiment: America wanted to believe that its daughters were models of Victorian modesty and that its sons presided lovingly over invariably happy households. Smile as we may at the dated naïveté of these lithographs and of the millions who bought them, they do bespeak a time when domestic pleasures were simply given and simply taken; in that there is strength, and perhaps they serve today to mock, in their gentle way, our mockery of them.*

THE LOVERS QUARREL.   THE LOVERS RECONCILIATION.

Nathaniel Currier and, later, James Merritt Ives held up a full-length mirror to the prevailing American interests and attitudes from 1834 until the turn of the present century. They offered colorful glimpses of every aspect of life—urban and rural scenes, catastrophes, political cartoons, portraits of the famous, historicals and sentimentals, views of railroads and rivers, sporting events and sailing ships—there were over seven thousand subjects in all. The bustling shop at 152 Nassau Street in New York (and the peddlers and travelling salesmen who carried its wares to the rest of the nation) held something for every taste and every pocketbook. Small prints like these were as little as six cents apiece wholesale; now, of course, they are, along with all the others in the repertoire, collectors' items that have restaked the claim of their creators to the proud republican title "Printmakers to the American People."

THE DAY BEFORE MARRIAGE.

THE WEDDING DAY.

THE HAPPY HOME.

Under way, the 224-foot Manhattan's decks were awash, and her crew had to remain below inside the hot, airless iron hull.

"this filthy ironpot"

Civil War ironclads were dirty, hot, cramped, and dangerously unseaworthy.
An officer's diary describes life aboard during the crucial Battle of Mobile Bay

By ROBERT B. ELY, *Acting Lieutenant, U.S.N.*

In the spring of 1864, Robert B. Ely, a twenty-three-year-old acting volunteer lieutenant in the United States Navy, was assigned to duty in the U.S.S. Manhattan, a single-turret, ironclad monitor fresh from the builder's yard at Jersey City. After meeting the usual problems that go with fitting a new crew into an untried ship, the Manhattan sailed for the Gulf of Mexico, and on August 5 it was with Rear Admiral David Glasgow Farragut's fleet in the momentous Battle of Mobile Bay.

Ely kept a private journal, and he found a good deal to write about. He distinguished himself in battle—apparently he was what would nowadays be called the gunnery officer— and he won promotion, along with assignment as his ship's executive officer. What makes his journal readable today, however, is not so much his account of a famous sea fight as his unvarnished story of what life on a Civil War monitor was really like.

That life, as he quickly discovered, was about as uncomfortable as any-

COLLECTION OF ROBERT B. ELY III

Lieutenant Ely

thing the Navy has ever had to offer. Those primitive ironclads were just barely seaworthy and almost completely uninhabitable. Simply living on a monitor was so trying that the ordeal of battle struck all hands as a positive relief.

At sea, the monitors were utter slugs, needing to be towed if they were to make any headway—the Manhattan made the entire trip from New York to Mobile Bay at one end of a towrope, the other end being attached to the stern of a wooden gunboat, the U.S.S. Bienville—and in action, when the tows were cast off, they were slow and very hard to steer. They were shotproof, but when a solid shot hit their armor, boltheads would snap off and fly about the interior in a most lethal manner. They had so little reserve buoyancy that a leak could be fatal, as one of the Manhattan's sister monitors, the U.S.S. Tecumseh, found when she struck a mine going into Mobile Bay.

But it was the day-to-day discom-

fort of life aboard that was the real problem. In anything but a flat calm, a monitor's deck was awash, so that the crew either had to stay below or go up on top of the turret, where most of the space was taken up by the conning tower. This meant that most of the men, whether on duty or off, had to stay below, and that was abominable because at sea the hatches were battened down and the ventilators were usually inoperative. The hot Gulf coast sun beat down on the iron deck, turning the interior into a veritable oven (Ely noted one time when the temperature in the engine room ran above 130 degrees), and the air in the living and working quarters was a thick fog that could hardly be breathed. Everything was wet, partly because of condensation from the humid air and partly because there was a constant seepage at the base of the turret; also, the wooden hull that carried the dead weight of armor plate "worked" hard and had a way of developing innumerable leaks.

Nevertheless, Farragut had to use monitors in order to win his battle. Mobile Bay was protected by three forts—the largest, Fort Morgan, on the east side of the entrance; Fort Gaines on the western side directly opposite; and Fort Powell covering a secondary entrance a few miles to the northwest. In addition, the Confederates had the C.S.S. Tennessee, a recently finished ironclad ram that was more than a match for the best wooden warships Farragut had. To win, Farragut had to pass the forts and silence the Tennessee and her consorts, three wooden gunboats. The gunboats he could handle, and he could rush past the forts the way he had rushed past the forts at New Orleans two years earlier, but the Tennessee was likely to checkmate him unless he had monitors. So he used four of them—the Manhattan, the unlucky Tecumseh, and two double-turret affairs named the Winnebago and the Chickasaw.

Ely had gone to sea on a merchant ship before the war. He entered the Navy in 1861, serving at various times on the warships Dana, Yankee, and Mohican. He was married not long before he sailed on the Manhattan, and—like men in the armed services in all wars—his morale depended largely on the frequency with which he got letters from his wife, Nellie.

His private journal is owned now by his grandson, Robert B. Ely III of Philadelphia. With his permission, portions of it are published here for the first time. Our excerpt begins on June 30, 1864, when the Manhattan was nearing Key West.   —Bruce Catton

The sea has been running quite high all day and . . . the ship presents a very strange appearance, almost ending submerged, the only dry spot being the turret about which the sea breaks and foams in impotent fury. Dr. Austin has been quite seasick all day. He wishes himself at home again and laments that he did not join the Army. It is generally understood on board today that we are bound to Pensacola, and from thence probably to Mobile. I hope we meet and annihilate the Tennessee.

One of our officers has been having a tent made which he has pitched over his berth as a kind of roof to shed the water, he not being sufficiently nautical in his tastes to admire the dripping of salt water on his person during his moments of repose. The wardroom is quite uncomfortable with streams of water trickling down from the deck above in all directions. One eccentric little timber drops directly on my head while seated at the table, thereby counteracting the great heat which I would otherwise experience, the thermometer being 90° F^ht. I think the government ought to furnish the officers of ironclads with a suit of storm clothes suitable to wear at "all times," a water cooler, and the most amiable disposition imaginable.

All our officers seem to bear their discomforts most philosophically, taking them as a matter of course and making speculations as to what will be the surest way to save their best suits of clothes if we should sink. Every evening we all take off every article of dress except our underclothing and abandon ourselves to a most luxurious "perspire."

July 1—The day has been so excessively hot that I am almost melted. The thermometer in the wardroom stands at 90°, while on deck the weather is very pleasant, a fair breeze blowing from the East. Everything is dirty, everything smells bad, everybody is demoralized. How are you, Ironclad? A man who would stay in an ironclad from choice is a candidate for the insane asylum, and he who stays from compulsion is an object of pity. Fresh leaks are breaking out every day . . . it is the result of stopping up some of the old ones. The Doctor and Paymaster have been chasing one leak backward and forward from one of their rooms to the other for several days. At one time I hear the Doctor complaining of it, the carpenter is called, the leak is stopped, and in a few hours I hear the Paymaster growling at the Doctor for driving it into his room, and vice versa.

July 2—This day has been worse than yesterday. It

was absolutely insupportable and this evening we have shipped the ventilator in spite of the wind or sea. This makes it possible for us to "exist" below. I can't imagine how the firemen and coalheavers stand it. The thermometer in the fireroom stands at 135° to 138°. The Chief Engineer goes in there semi-occasionally to superintend the work and comes out again wringing wet, [cursing] all the ironclad fleet.

We have been passing beacons and lighthouses all day and expect to put into Key West some time tomorrow morning. I suppose we will soon be at our journey's end and then for a try with the *Tennessee*. I understand that it is a powerful vessel and will probably stand a good deal of punishment.

I hope we will finish here in quick order and leave for some other port where we can make a better

match of it. While we are obliged to lay out in the open roadstead, we will probably be obliged to keep our hatches battened down and be absolutely roasted alive. Three months' service in an ironclad ought to insure a man's promotion to a brigadier general.

July 3—This morning at 6 o'clock we arrived at Key West, not a very promising looking place. The most remarkable feature from the sea view is Fort Taylor.

The time is shortly after 7:15 A.M. on August 5, 1864, and the battle for Mobile Bay has just begun. Farragut's fleet—fourteen wooden cruisers lashed together in pairs and four ironclads—is drawing abreast of Fort Morgan. The Admiral's flag flies in Hartford, *starboard ship of the second pair. The ironclads—*Tecumseh (*sinking after striking a mine*), *Manhattan (*Lieutenant Ely's ship*), *Winnebago, *and* Chickasaw—*are inshore to protect the cruisers against the armored ram* Tennessee, *steaming toward them with two gunboats as escorts.*

. . . There is a Naval Club established here of which our first lieutenant is a member. Some of the other members have been on board today. They gave a very lively description of the state of society here. . . . Among the ladies, naval officers are in such high repute that whenever one dies in their station at least *one* lady on the island goes into mourning for him, asserting that she was his affianced bride, and that Death alone has separated them.

The yellow fever is raging here to a fearful extent. The Admiral of the Squadron is at present very low with this fearful disease. We will take in a little coal here and then leave for parts unknown. . . .

July 4—This day I spent without much of the excitement attendant upon the anniversary of the Declaration of Independence. I got up at 4 A.M. and prepared to take in coal and was hard at work until 8 A.M., getting the ship ready for sea and putting the coal aboard. At 10 we got under weigh and bid Key West a fond adieu, bound for the Dry Tortugas, a distance of 60 miles. We expect to arrive there about 8 this evening, remain there a few hours, then off for Pensacola. It is now a certain thing that Mobile is our place of destination. . . .

The wardroom today is quite comfortable, the thermometer standing at 68°. I was foolish enough to put on a pair of white pants this morning. Before the work had stopped they were all the colors of the rainbow, ironrust and green being predominant. . . . At 8 we made Tortugas Light.

July 5—We have been favored with unusually fine weather since we joined this vessel, having had no heavy blows and not one rain storm. Anything but bad weather in an ironclad. We are obliged to live on deck at sea and if it rains it makes it very disagreeable. . . . I can't help envying the officers of the *Bienville*. We can see her decks very plainly. Everything is neat and clean and the officers are nicely dressed, and look as comfortable as possible. I suppose they have their own fun at our expense, seeing us all crowded up on the turret, looking over the iron railing, with wistful glances at the deck, like a lot of old hens with broods of ducks who persist in going into the water.

July 6—. . . Our men have never been drilled yet, and being the officer in command of the turret and guns I do not feel altogether satisfied about it but perhaps I shall do better than I anticipated when the time comes. The drill is very simple and in a fight I trust a great deal to the good sense of the gun's crews. We broke out and whitewashed the hold under the wardroom this afternoon, and find that it makes the air much more pure. Too much care cannot be taken aboard an ironclad to keep her clean.

July 7—This afternoon at 1:20 made Pensacola light-house and came to our anchor in the harbor of the Navy Yard. We at once took off our hatches and allowed fresh air to circulate fully through the ship. The wardroom is like a different place this evening. We have cleared our decks of all lumber and are now ready for action. The Admiral is at Mobile to which place we will proceed as soon as some few slight repairs to the engine are completed. I suppose we will soon have our reckoning with the *Tennessee*. . . .

I wrote a letter to Nellie this evening but the mail left in such a short time after our arrival that I had only time enough to state our safe arrival and wish her health and happiness. We have regular mail communication between the Gulf and New York twice a week and I promise myself the pleasure of hearing from my dear wife very often during the time I may be attached to this squadron. . . .

July 9—We have been busy all day taking in coal, getting provisions aboard, etc. The weather has been excessively warm and I have been very uncomfortable in consequence thereof. . . . We are very much in want of fresh provisions and vegetables. In consequence of an order issued by the Admiral forbidding all communications between the ship and the shore we are unable to do any marketing. . . .

July 10—Excessively hot all day. At 10 inspected the crew at general quarters. Read them the Riot Act, etc. At 11 the Captain [Commander J. W. A. Nicholson] conducted divine services on the quarter deck. We have been visited by officers and men from several of ships lying in the harbor. All seem to think that a fight between this vessel and the *Tennessee* is a settled thing as soon as we arrive off Mobile. We have all been having a social chat on the quarter deck this evening with our shirt collars unbuttoned, chairs pitched back, feet on the life lines and pipes in a cheerful glow, to keep away the mosquitoes. . . . In the intervals of silence I thought of my dear little wife, far away, and wished I could be spending this Sabbath evening in her dear company. I suppose the single gentlemen are thinking of their sweethearts and visions of them and other dear ones are now floating in the clouds of smoke before the eyes of us all. . . .

July 12—Fine weather all day. Have been visited by several parties of ladies and gentlemen. We had got the ship all nicely cleaned, coaled, and provisioned ready for sea, when just at luncheon the alarming cry of "The ship's on fire!" was heard from the engine room. All hands were at once called to fire quarters, pumps were rigged and we had our fire buckets get to work. We closed all the air ports, hatches, smoke stacks and every opening by which any draught could get to the fire. All the officers and men worked with a will and at 11 o'clock we had the fire well under com-

Tecumseh: Then and Now

A light breeze had dissipated the last wisps of a lingering fog and was ushering in a clear, sunny August morning as the ironclad monitor *Tecumseh* led the line of Union warships up the channel and into the Battle of Mobile Bay. At 6:45 the *Tecumseh* fired the first shot, a range-seeking 15-inch shell that exploded over Fort Morgan. Half an hour later the ironclad was at the narrowest part of the passage; only a few hundred yards separated the Scylla of the fort and the Charybdis of the field of submerged "torpedoes." The Federals were aware of the mines, even to knowing that a certain red buoy marked the edge of their farthest encroachment into the channel. But, either to keep as far as possible from the menacing parapets or to maneuver for an encounter with the approaching Confederate ram *Tennessee,* Captain Tunis A. M. Craven ordered the *Tecumseh* to swing inside the crucial buoy. Detonating a mine, the ironclad lurched and sank posthaste, carrying with her Craven and ninety-two others. Of the twenty-one survivors, seventeen were picked up by Union ships; four swam to shore and were cap-

Magruder and Tecumseh's *anchor*

tured. The *Tecumseh*'s pilot, John Collins, lived to relate an incident that made Craven a hero. Just after the explosion, the two met at the foot of the ladder leading up through the turret to safety. Craven, as if to say Collins was not at fault, said, "After you, pilot." Collins ascended and found "there was nothing after me; when I reached the upmost round of the

ladder, the vessel seemed to drop from under me."

The Smithsonian Institution and the Navy's Department of Salvage are undertaking to raise the *Tecumseh* from her 103-year sleep on the muddy floor of Mobile Bay and to give her a permanent berth in Washington, D.C. The project's overseer is Colonel John H. Magruder III, director of the National Armed Forces Museum Advisory Board, who is shown at the left with an anchor retrieved from the ironclad shortly after she was located and positively identified in February of 1967. (Incidentally, Colonel Magruder is the son of the late Commodore Magruder, seen accepting the Japanese surrender of the Bonin Islands in a photograph on page 62.) The salvage job, still in the planning stages, must be executed with extreme delicacy: there is a trove of artifacts encased in the *Tecumseh,* and the hull will have to undergo desalinization to reacclimate the metal to the atmosphere. But once she breaks surface and is relocated —Magruder hopes by 1970—it will have been worth the time and expense, for the *Tecumseh* will be the only extant specimen of a Civil War monitor, the antecedent of today's fighting ships.

---

mand. Several of the officers fainted from heat and exhaustion. I escaped with only a slight stifling and a bad headache. . . .

July 13—Today all hands have been employed cleaning away the muck left by the fire. I was called into the cabin this morning by the Captain and told emphatically that he was very much dissatisfied with the manner in which the First Lieutenant carried on the duties of the ship, stating that he was dirty, disorganized, etc.; said he was fully satisfied that I was in every way qualified to carry out the executive duty of the ship to his satisfaction, and asked me if I was willing to undertake it. I told him that I was. He said that he was going on board the flagship and would at once make application for another ensign in place of our present 1st Lt., and ask that he might be detached.

I am sorry for some reasons, and of course I am glad for others that the case stands as it does. Whether I shall succeed remains to be seen after I have made the attempt. There are a great many things aboard an ironclad to discourage a first lieutenant, but yet I think a strict attention to duty will carry him safely through. For the present, things remain in status quo.

Ely's assignment as executive officer was finally made, but not until after the battle of Mobile Bay.

July 15—. . . Carpenters and mechanics generally have been at work on board all day, repairing the damage done by the fire. I have been patiently waiting ever since I came aboard this vessel to see her cleaned and made at least respectable. This happy end has not yet been attained and she remains in the most filthy condition. There is no system, no order. All is confusion.

CONTINUED ON PAGE 108

Is this any way to ruin a

America's railway tycoons had decided that it was much more profitable to move freight than people long before the Great Northern's president, James J. Hill, scornfully compared a passenger train to "the male teat—neither useful nor ornamental." This self-defeating attitude, explored by Peter Lyon in our essay on pages 2–3, persists today, in the face of a growing urban transportation morass that threatens to make our cities uninhabitable and often unreachable. Traffic clogs the proliferating freeways and parking lots faster than they can be built. Fumes pollute our air, and noise makes day and night hideous around our overcrowded airports. In the following excerpt from his current book, To Hell in a Day Coach: An Exasperated Look at American Railroads, *Mr. Lyon issues a polemic in behalf of the bedevilled railway passenger. Against a backdrop of historic managerial greed and stupidity, he probes the callous deceit and disregard for the public interest that still characterize the approach of most of our railroads toward the passenger train at the very moment in our history when it seems needed the most.* —The Editors

In the face of the stubborn contrariety of the railroad managers, the notion has begun to take hold that the best way of travelling between cities a few hundred miles apart—the most efficient, cheapest, most convenient, surest, safest, and potentially the most comfortable—is the way that has been available for a hundred years or more: the railway.

Proponents of this notion are not, of course, plumping for railroad passenger service as we know it today —the slow, dirty, noisy, unpunctual, inconvenient jouncing about that is contemptuously provided in dilapidated equipment. What they have in mind is a smooth, comfortable ride at speeds up to 150 miles an hour, regularly available in pleasant, modern coaches and parlor cars—no more than could and should have been provided since 1946 or thereabouts, if the officers of the railroad companies had been alert to the public interest and aggressive in competing for the public custom; no more than what has in fact been provided in Canada, in Japan, and in Europe,

which means by railroads that have been nationalized.

Until quite recently, such a notion has been poison to the directors of American railroads, and most of them still regard it as a threat to all they hold dear. For at least a generation all of them have, for sundry reasons, persistently sought to scuttle most of their passenger service, and some of them have contrived to slaughter their passenger business entirely. There has been nothing sly or underhanded about this policy; on the contrary, it has been plugged diligently by the presidents of the biggest and most influential railroad companies. As long ago as July, 1956, Donald J. Russell, then the president of the Southern Pacific, in an interview with a reporter of the San Francisco *Chronicle,* cheerfully predicted the demise of the Pullman car and the virtual extinction of long-distance travel on rails; he acknowledged that most railroads would like to get out of the passenger business completely. A month later, James M. Symes, then the president of the Pennsylvania, told a reporter of the *New York Times:* "I've just about given up hope as to the future of long-haul passenger travel." These gentlemen were not so much advocating as describing a process that had been in full swing since 1929 (when Class I railroads boasted 47,797 passenger cars rolling over 266,-703 miles of track) and would proceed even more swiftly after they had spoken (until by 1966 a mere 10,687 passenger cars would operate on 72,796 miles of passenger-service tracks).

Precise figures for intercity passenger trains, as distinct from commuter trains, are difficult to come by, but in 1929 there were at least twenty thousand of them. In September, 1965, Wayne Hoffman, the executive vice president of the New York Central, estimated that their number had dwindled from eleven thousand in 1946 to thirteen hundred in 1964. As of August, 1967, there were less than nine hundred. At least two states and several sizable cities had no railroad passenger service whatsoever. There was no through service between Washington and Cleveland, Cleveland and Detroit, Cleveland and Pittsburgh, Detroit and Indianapolis, St. Louis and Louisville, Atlanta and Jacksonville, or Dallas and San Antonio.

railroad?

You bet it is, say the railway moguls, who in fifty years almost managed to get rid of the "passenger element." Then a freshman senator derailed them with a plan to keep the day coaches rolling

By PETER LYON

Efforts to discontinue service between New York and Boston and to reduce service between San Francisco and Los Angeles have been, at least for a time, rejected.

To the directors of most railroad companies, this was a very satisfactory state of affairs. They were content. One could almost hear them purr as, through the 1960's, the Dow-Jones average of railroad stocks maintained a jagged ascent. These men had only to close their eyes and count to ten; when they opened their eyes again—presto! chango!—the passenger business would have vanished; or so they hoped. But instead they began to hear talk of a rejuvenated passenger service. Their exasperation can be imagined.

The talk was started by a few dreamy, meddlesome scholars—professors of urban planning or of transportation who should have known better. They were ignored; after all, their voices could not carry very far.

But then an imaginative politician spoke up, one who actually preferred the railroad for travel back and forth between Washington and his constituency and so was vividly aware of all the railroad's shortcomings and all its wasted potentials. Claiborne Pell, the junior senator from Rhode Island, after pondering these shortcomings, went so far as to draft a set of simple specific proposals for the resuscitation of railroad passenger service, at least in the northeastern states. Pell was new to the Senate (he was first elected in 1960), but he was no stranger to men of considerable influence. He took his plan to an old friend, Arthur Krock, the Washington commentator for the *New York Times*, who at once appreciated the right of the matter: the Pell plan was reported on the front page of the newspaper on May 21, 1962.

In the executive offices of several railroad companies, that Monday morning was a bleak one. All along the Atlantic seaboard, railroad directors were recalling the words of the poet Burns about the best-laid schemes of mice and men. The president of one great eastern railroad system picked up his telephone and spoke forcefully to Pell for a half hour, seeking to dissuade him from his foolish notion of an improved rail passenger service. Too late. Within ten days the editors of ten big newspapers published in the northeastern states had jumped, with glad cries, aboard the Pell bandwagon; and before long the editors of half a dozen railway labor weeklies were whooping their approval. A public debate on intercity railroad passenger service had been assured.

For years before it was moved into the arena of public policy, the debate had been conducted in the pages of such trade magazines as *Trains, Railway Age,* and *Modern Railroads;* and it had boiled over, too, at nearly every public hearing called (by the Interstate

"*This model features worn-out equipment, which causes excitingly real hotboxes, delays, and other true-to-life malfunctions.*"

Commerce Commission or by one of the state regulatory agencies) to judge whether specific passenger trains might be discontinued. A salient aspect of the debate was the attempt to fix responsibility for the calamitous decline of the service in the face of a growing population and an expanding travel market.

The lords of the railroads have had no difficulty in identifying those responsible for the loss of their passengers, and they seem honestly bewildered that anyone else could hesitate to do so. They point, in summary fashion, to the automobile and the airplane, and to the distressful manner in which those competitors have been pampered and cosseted by politicians at every level from the county courthouse to the White House, all to the ruinous detriment of the railroads. Moreover, evidence abounds to back up their lamentations. In the 1950's the federal, state, and local governments spent hundreds of millions of dollars each year to build highways and airports and in other ways to promote and subsidize travel by airplane or automobile. In the 1960's more than one billion dollars a year have gone to beef up air transport and more than ten billion a year to build still more highways. Some part of these monstrous sums—perhaps as much as two thirds of them—has been recovered by excise taxes on gasoline, tires, and the like, or by tolls and other imposts levied on those who choose to use the highways or the airways; but the vast remainder has been extracted from the general taxpayer, including, of course, the railroad company.

To the railroad operators it seemed quite clear that their passengers were quitting them for the swifter airplane and the more convenient private automobile, and that the Interstate Commerce Commission and the various state regulatory agencies were nevertheless forcing them to maintain an unpopular, archaic, and hideously expensive service. There could be no question that the costs of the service were climbing dizzily. In the early postwar years, the cost of labor rose from almost $200,000,000 for 42,850 passenger service employees in 1947, to $179,000,000 for 16,767 employees in 1966.

This pay is based upon work rules that have been in force since 1919. For engine crews, the rule reads: "One hundred miles or less (straightaway or turnaround) ... shall constitute a day's work; miles in excess of one hundred will be paid for at the mileage rate provided." For conductors and trainmen a day's work is one hundred and fifty miles or less (straightaway or turnaround). Engine crew and train crew alike are paid overtime "on a speed basis of twenty miles per hour computed continuously from the time required to report for duty until released at the end of the last run." Since 1919 the average speed of passenger trains has somewhat increased, so that "a day's work" has diminished from about five hours to about three hours and twenty minutes.

Translated into operational examples, this means that the New York Central must employ eight engine crews, whose members divide about nine and one-half basic days' pay, to move its Twentieth Century nine hundred and sixty miles between New York and Chicago, or that the Burlington must employ eight engine crews, whose members divide ten and one-third basic days' pay, to move its Denver Zephyr about one thousand miles between Denver and Chicago.

The Interstate Commerce Commission, using an antique statistical formula of its own contrivance, concluded in 1957 that the passenger service had for the previous seven years saddled the railroads with an annual deficit of more than five hundred million dollars. Since many of the biggest railroad companies were suffused with red ink at the time, their officers indicted the traffic in passengers as an intolerable burden. On cue, spokes-

"I just never imagined they wouldn't finally come up with some form of government aid."

54

men for the shippers likewise began to yowl that the passenger-train deficits were crippling the railroads and preventing them from the efficient discharge of their divine duty: to wit, the carriage of freight.

Responsive to these protests, the commission undertook to investigate the passenger-train deficit. The hearings ambled along, like an accommodation local, from June 18, 1957, to June 23, 1958 (while the deficit itself, by the commission's intricate formula of accounting, mounted in 1957 to an all-time record of $724,000,000); they served to convince at least the hearings examiner, Howard Hosmer, who predicted, "the parlor and sleeping-car service will have disappeared by 1965 and the coach service by 1970."

That was precisely what most (but by no means all) lords of the railroads had hoped would be predicted. They had already besought Congress for relief, and in August, 1958, they had got it. An amendment (Section 13a) to the Interstate Commerce Act put a gratifying zip into the process by which passenger trains, whether interstate or intrastate, could be forever curtailed, cancelled, and discontinued. The extermination picked up speed and proceeded merrily apace—until all at once Senator Pell's consarned plan burst into the public prints. Since then, the extermination has proceeded, but cautiously, more slowly, with greater difficulty, for now the other side of the debate has been given a hearing and respectful attention.

The opposition holds that the lords of the railroads are solely responsible for the deterioration of the passenger service, just as they have always been responsible for the uncivil and contemptuous treatment that has been the passenger's traditional lot on most railroads. This argument has never been articulated or documented with as much skill as has the railroads' argument, but at no time in the history of American railroads have passengers failed to remark the singular reluctance of railroad presidents to afford comfortable, even minimally decent accommodations. Whatever provides ease or convenience may subtract from financial profit, and the railroad president has ever been spurred by his natural greed for profit.

The first truly radical change in the manufacture of railroad cars, when wood was replaced by steel, was made in 1894; it began, logically enough from the standpoint of the railroads, with freight cars. Not until fourteen years later, in 1908, did the Pullman-Standard Car Manufacturing Company begin production of all-steel passenger cars. The company was obliged to make this extraordinary decision because of the very real hazard that steam locomotives, puffing up clouds of glowing sparks, might set afire the old wooden coaches if they were hauled through the

tunnel the Pennsylvania was then building (to be opened in 1910) under the Hudson River from New Jersey to New York City.

The all-steel sleeping car came later, making a modest appearance in 1910 and no considerable splash until the mid-1920's, when passenger revenues from Pullman cars were at their zenith. This was the car now considered high camp, the car that evokes memories of the romantic Nights of the Green Curtains. Only those of us who are in our forties or older can recall those sleepers, characterized so aptly as "rolling tenements." They were ugly, uncomfortable dormitories, as lacking in privacy as a jailhouse. Each passenger rocked longitudinally in a berth cloaked only by a swaying curtain of a heavy dark-green fabric that might better have been used as an upholstery for the furniture in the lobbies of commercial hotels. At one end of each sleeper was the men's room—one toilet, a pseudo-leathern couch, and a meager triad of communal washbasins, inadequately equipped with mirrors, in front of which a gaggle of salesmen customarily postured and prattled, exchanging jokes of an unexampled vulgarity; at the other end was the women's room—similarly fitted, and littered with someone else's face powder and someone else's hair combings.

Spurred by concern for the comfort of their passengers, the railroad executives required that three improvements be made in these hideous sleeping cars: In 1924 receptacles for used razor blades were installed in the men's rooms. In 1926 containers of fresh facial tissues were placed in some, but not all, of the women's rooms. In 1929 the water coolers were adjusted so that they would no longer overflow on the strip of carpeting in the corridors.

There was also the matter of air conditioning. One would think that the lords of the railroads would have snatched at air conditioning when it first became practical; would, even more likely, have themselves been first to conceive of it; for surely there are few surroundings in which the human being can more gratefully welcome a constant supply of cooled, clean air than a railroad coach drawn by a steam locomotive on a hot day. With windows closed, the passengers baked; with windows opened (presuming, of course, that someone had the Herculean strength required to open a coach window), the passengers were aspersed with soot and grime and coal dust, and their lungs filled with a noxious stench.

Yet long after the feasibility of air-conditioned passenger trains had been demonstrated, the railroad operators hung back. In concert, they declined to install the necessary devices; all their available funds were bespoken by their investment bankers, who were advising them in their financially calamitous ventures in the stock market. Not until their passenger revenues fell off sharply, after 1929, did they turn to air conditioning, and then they could ill afford it; not until late into the 1930's were most trains routinely equipped with air-conditioned passenger cars; and a few of the smaller roads waited until 1950 to begin granting their customers this minimal comfort.

The conclusion is inescapable that the general public, badly used by the railroads from the first day a flanged wheel rolled along an iron rail, could not wait for the opportunity to use another mode of travel. They had been fighting bitterly for nearly a century; now they wanted only to switch.

Belatedly a few railroads, especially those in the West, set out to recapture their passengers. In 1934 the Union Pacific put on a lightweight train that cut the time between Chicago and Los Angeles from sixty to less than forty hours; the Burlington began operating its swift, handsome Zephyrs; and in 1935 the Santa Fe was obliged to schedule lightweight trains of its own. Industrial designers were retained who made the first changes in the design of sleeping cars and lounge cars since the time, back in the 1870's, when those elegant creatures had first been built. For the New York Central, Henry Dreyfuss redesigned the Twentieth Century, Raymond Loewy did the same for the Pennsylvania's Broadway Limited, and curious crowds gathered in the big New York depots of both roads to examine sleeping cars which, for a wonder, afforded privacy: drawing rooms, sections, bedrooms, compartments that gave each traveller a washbasin and a toilet of his own and a door that he could lock. Was it possible? It was possible, but it had come too late. Of the rich and fastidious, fewer would patronize these expensive cars each year; and the masters of the railroads had ignored, in their calculations, the scores of millions of other travelling Americans who had turned to the bus.

The bus, the noisome bus. It was typical of the footling way the railroads had operated their passenger service that an inelegant carrier like the bus should have emerged as a rival able to cut deep into the revenues of the noble railroad; able to ring up half as many passenger-miles as the railroads by 1940.

With the connivance of the railroads, who for many years invested heavily in bus company stocks, the passengers left the trains for the bus. Their departure gave the railroads in turn another excuse to drop their branch lines. More passengers left for the automobile and, slowly at first, for the airplane. Yet more railroad executives persisted in proceeding as though the railroad still enjoyed a monopoly. If there has

emerged a glaring contradiction, the explanation is that we are here dealing with the railroad industry.

A revolution was in full cycle, but the railroad managers, hidebound as ever, failed to measure its sweep. In retrospect, one can understand why they were so blinded, even while losing patience with them for their refusal to open their eyes to what was going on around them. The depression of the 1930's threatened to engulf almost every railroad company in ultimate disaster; the war of the early 1940's buried every railroad under an avalanche of traffic. During those fifteen years the managers of the railroads were so absorbed by their immediate concerns that they never paused to learn from the lessons of yesterday or to consider the possible exigencies of tomorrow.

Incredible as it may seem, when in 1946 the railroad managers began to struggle with the postwar problems of their passenger service, they knew almost nothing about their market or about the flow and pattern of traffic.

Into this dark abysm of assumption and conjecture the railroad men bravely plunged. They were certain of only one fact: their passenger cars were old, shabby, and in dreadful disrepair; so, they spent with a free hand. More than $500,000,000 in the five years from 1946 to 1950 went to buy more than 4,000 new passenger-train cars—handsome, expensive, air-conditioned, and built according to the traditional heavyweight design to last for at least a generation. Yet in each year the number of their passengers dwindled.

In the next five years they spent their money more cautiously. Less than $250,000,000 went to purchase new equipment, and of that sum a larger share was paid to buy cars for the so-called head-end traffic—that is, cars built to haul mail and baggage and express freight. Yet in each year the number of passengers diminished. Could it be that they had somehow overlooked some aspect of their passenger service?

During these same five years the Pennsylvania, the New York Central, and the Baltimore & Ohio engaged Robert Heller Associates, consultants on problems of management, to inquire into the habits and preferences of passengers on every train east of the Mississippi and the Missouri, north from the Gulf of Mexico into the Maritime Provinces of Canada. Here was the most comprehensive and thoroughgoing study ever undertaken for any mode of transportation in the history of the Republic. It cost about five million dollars. Motivation of travellers, operation of trains, costs and marketing of the passenger service—all this and much more was painstakingly investigated. The purpose of the study was to enable the directors of the three railroads to determine the feasibility of consolidating their passenger services. (Think what might have come to pass: a rational integration of terminals and depots, a saving of millions of dollars by elimination of unnecessary competition, a more frequent and more convenient schedule of trains, cheaper fares, swifter, more comfortable rides; in short, a paradise for those who prefer to travel by train in the overcrowded eastern region.) Nothing happened. The study itself, an invaluable research, was discarded, scattered, or destroyed; not maliciously, not with evil intent, but (as I have been told by one of those familiar with the research) only stupidly, only because the executives who had it in charge knew no better.

"They're making a little too much of this bankruptcy business."

Much interest attached to a few of the cars built at this time, for these few, which cost less than ten million dollars, were genuine innovations in passenger equipment, proudly hailed as "the trains of the future"—streamlined, built of lightweight aluminum or stainless steel, and manufactured to run in fixed sets of six or eight or a dozen cars. They bore flamboyant names like Aerotrain and X-Plorer and RDC-Hot Rod. They were hurried into service early in 1956 and almost immediately proved to be a resounding flop. They trembled and shook at high speed; they were noisy; they broke down easily and often, but their sets could not be readily parted to detach an intermediate car for repair or maintenance; they could not be interchanged with cars of traditional design; they were too light to trip the devices that activated signal systems. By 1960 they had all been scrapped or relegated to service on suburban runs, and the whole episode had perfectly demonstrated what the venerable dodoes of the industry had known all along, to wit: "Never monkey around with damnfool experiments." . . . "The old way is the best way." . . . "Whatever is old has been tested by time."

The masters of the railroads now reformed their ranks in a sullen phalanx. What they had never properly understood they now condemned. Even before the new lightweight equipment had proved to be a costly mistake, the Eastern Railroad Presidents Conference was urged to seek a steep increase in passenger fares and especially in Pullman fares. This plan was proposed by the New York Central and heartily endorsed by the Pennsylvania. (The other eastern carriers at first declined to support it.) The plan was revealed on July 25, 1956, by a knowledgeable reporter of railroad affairs, Robert Bedingfield, in an article published on the front page of the *New York Times*. The headline put it neatly: 2 RAILWAYS PLAN FARE RISE TO DETER PULLMAN TRAVEL. Just in case some reader might have missed the import of the headline, the president of a smaller railroad was quoted in unmistakable terms: "What they are trying to do is to dry up the Pullman service and switch the passengers over to the coach and the airplane." In fine, the big railroads hoped to use the fare—the rate for passengers—as an instrument of policy to club their ratepayers into doing as they wished.

There were other ways, in 1956, to enervate the passenger service. Advertising budgets, already minuscule, could be reduced still further. In 1946 the industry had submitted to a little self-criticism on this score from its creature, the Association of American Railroads. "Railroads," the A.A.R. said in a report on passenger traffic, "spend insignificant sums for advertising in comparison with the amount of business done," and the report went on to point out that even in 1943, when travel by the domestic airlines was constantly jeopardized by military priorities, the airlines had spent twenty-five times as much (in relation to revenues) as had the railroads, in trying to drum up their passenger business. But after 1950, instead of beefing up their advertising of passenger services, most railroad companies cut it to the bone and deeper, into the marrow. They even rejected a successful experimental method of increasing revenues by paying sales commissions to ticket agents.

CONTINUED ON PAGE 78

THE BONINS—ISLES OF

Matthew Calbraith Perry, the Great Commodore, home again in 1855 after his celebrated expedition to the Far East, brought with him not only a treaty of friendship linking the United States and Japan but also a powerful vision of what the future held for the seas between. "It is not to be supposed," he wrote, "that the numberless islands which lie scattered throughout this immense ocean are always to remain unproductive, and under the mismanagement of savages. The history of the world forbids any such conclusion. How, and in what way, the aborigines will be disposed of—whether by just or unjust means—cannot be known at the present time; but that they are doomed to mingle with, or give way to some other race, is as certain as the fate of our own melancholy red brethren."

Perry believed as an article of faith that his countrymen should take the lead in shaping the destiny of the Pacific, and he directed their attention to one place in particular among the numberless islands of the ocean—the Bonins. "In no part of the earth," he wrote, "can be found a more prolific soil than in those parts of the Bonins that have been brought into thorough cultivation." Perry proposed an American settlement there. A joint stock company could recruit young married couples and take them to their new home in whaling ships which would then cruise the Japan whaling grounds, returning loaded with oil. The Bonins would become a haven for shipping, and in addition they might serve as a base for American missionary work in Japan, Formosa, and other "benighted countries in that quarter of the globe."

Anyone who took the trouble to find this prospective outpost of America on a map of the Western Pacific might have been pardoned for doubting Perry's good sense. The Bonin Islands looked like nothing so much as a cartographer's mistake, part of a tiny ink spatter left by some draftsman who took great pains over the coast of Japan and then absent-mindedly flicked his pen dry in a line running south from Tokyo Bay toward Micronesia, across seas wracked by typhoons and tidal waves. The largest of the Bonins is less than ten square miles in size, and most of the others are just rocks and reefs, stretching away to the Izus in the north and the Volcanoes in the south.

Perry knew all this and discounted it. He had begun thinking seriously about the Bonins even before his expedition got under way; nothing he saw in the Far East led him to change his mind, and he came home more convinced than ever that he was right. In preparation for his voyage he had read everything he could find on Japan and the neighboring islands, and he had talked to New Englanders who had been in the Western Pacific. He knew about typhoons and tidal waves, but other considerations seemed to him more important. Between the Bonins and the southeastern coast of Japan flowed the Kuroshio, or Japan Current, an oceanic stream of warm water five hundred miles wide, sweeping northward at thirty or forty miles a day. Migrating whales and seals followed the Kuroshio, and for the American hunters who followed the herds, the Bonins were a useful place of refreshment. Then, too, the islands lay close to the great circle route from the Hawaiian Islands to the Chinese coastal city of Shanghai. Perry, one of the Navy's pioneers in the development of steam power, looked forward to the day when steamships would cross the Pacific from the west coast of America to the Orient, stopping for coal at Honolulu and then again at the Bonins. He was careful to see that all these ideas found their way into the published record of his expedition, and in the last years of his life he developed to the full his propaganda in behalf of American strategic, commercial, and moral influence in the Pacific, making sure that the Bonins were given a prominent place.

As far as Perry could see, no nation had a good claim to sovereignty there, and if that was the case then America should lead the way. While he was in the Far East he had been all for taking possession of the Bonins and holding on to them by the "best means," whatever these should turn out to be. He was far ahead of his time. When he died in 1858, the United States was scarcely a Pacific power, and it was not until the end of World War II that the Bonins came under official American administration. By that

CONTENTION

Americans settled early on the tiny, strategic Pacific islands, and dominate them again today. But the Japanese want them back

By TIMOTHY E. HEAD
and GAVAN DAWS

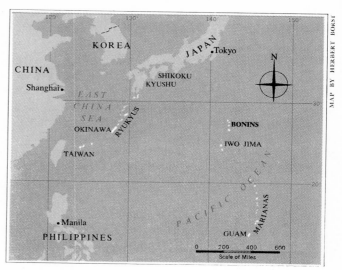

The Bonins' strategic location is clear from a simple map. Seen from the air (below), Chichi Jima, the largest island, is a green sickle against the blue ocean. Only about ten square miles in area, it still provides an excellent harbor, and the hillsides sloping back from the coast are richly fertile.

KYODO PHOTO SERVICE

time the strategic value of the islands went far beyond their use as fuel stations, a fact equally apparent to Japan and the United States, so that the question of the Bonins is still not settled in 1968.

Very few people shared Perry's enthusiasm for these insignificant islands. Spanish ships in the sixteenth century may have sighted them, and Dutch navigators plotted their location accurately in 1639, but not until the nineteenth century did Europeans go ashore there.

The Japanese knew the Bonins existed, but they had been turning their backs on the Pacific for centuries. They used their own closest southern outliers, the Izus, as a dumping ground for political criminals and other undesirables; the Bonins, only a few hundred miles farther out to sea, might just as well have been on the other side of the earth. From time to time junks in distress fetched up there, and their crews hurried to build new boats and go home. Occasionally a well-equipped expedition would be proposed, and one or two actually sailed, but the only result was the naming of the islands. A Japanese named Shimaya Ichizaemon spent several months ashore in 1675, and perhaps to compensate for the fact that he found no one living there, he turned the main islands themselves into a family. The northern cluster he named Bridegroom Island (Muko Jima), Bride, and Matchmaker. The central cluster's biggest island became Father Island (Chichi Jima), and three smaller ones, Elder Brother, Younger Brother, and Grandson. The southern cluster he called Mother Island (Haha Jima), Elder Sister, Younger Sister, and Niece. On his return to Japan, Shimaya confirmed earlier reports that the islands were *mun-in* or *bun-in,* empty of men. The group became known in the western world by a corruption of the latter term, Bonin.

In the eighteen twenties whaleships began to comb the Western Pacific north of the Equator, and in 1824 and 1825 an American, James Coffin of Nantucket, visited the southern, central, and northern clusters of the Bonins in the British whaler *Transit.* In 1826, another British whaler, the *William,* ran on the rocks and sank in the harbor at Chichi Jima. Most of her crew left aboard another ship, but two sailors named Wittrein and Peterson stayed behind to salvage the *William*'s cargo, a job made easier for them by a huge tidal wave that washed parts of the wreck a good way inland.

Wittrein and Peterson set themselves up in plank houses built from the debris of their ship, and they were eating well off hog meat and vegetables from their garden by the time the next visitors appeared, in June, 1827. H.M.S. *Blossom,* commanded by Frederick William Beechey, was the first man-of-war to anchor at Chichi Jima. Without making too much of

Obana Sakunosuke, first governor of the Bonins under the Japanese, in 1862, was an accomplished water-colorist. The Japanese inscription dimly visible on the hillside to the right of the ship in his view of Chichi Jima's harbor (top, left) reads: "Site bought by Perry as United States coaling station." Top, right, the Kanrin Maru passes an American whaling ship in Bonin waters. Above, a Japanese surveying party visits Tokoyo-No-Taki ("Eternity") Falls, one of the islands' lovely inland spots. Right, "Dance-jumping barbarian [non-Japanese] girls." They probably were half-American.

Three distinct phases in the twentieth-century history of the Bonins are represented by these three pictures. Horace and Benjamin Savory, sons of the American patriarch who settled there in 1830, pose with three of their descendants in 1926; Lieutenant

it, Beechey claimed the Bonins for Great Britain. "Taking possession of uninhabited islands," he wrote, "is now a mere matter of form; still I could not allow so fair an opportunity to escape, and declared them to be the property of the British government."

Beechey named the central cluster after himself, its principal island—Chichi Jima—Peel Island, and the harbor there Port Lloyd. He offered Wittrein and Peterson passage home, but they chose to stay awhile. Wittrein even toyed with the idea of living permanently on Peel Island. He had a house with a sign that read "Charles Wittrein's premises," a gun, a Bible, and a volume of the Encyclopedia Britannica, and he was thinking of getting a wife from Hawaii. For some reason he gave up this scheme and left with Peterson in 1828 on the next ship that came, the Russian man-of-war *Seniavin*.

At the end of the eighteen twenties, then, the Bonins had been sighted and visited by ships of several nations, and they belonged to Great Britain, but only as a "matter of form." In 1830 a small colonizing expedition was put together at Honolulu. The British consul there gave the settlers a Union Jack and his vague blessing. Beyond that he did nothing to help them, and he did not bother to report the venture to his home government. In his only letter on the subject of the Bonins, written eighteen months after the expedition set out, he merely mentioned that the islands might be useful "if colonized."

The leader of the settlers was Matteo Mozarro, an Italian who claimed to be a British subject. Mozarro

was something of a flag waver for his adopted country, but he did not, or could not, recruit only Britishers. His four fellow settlers were an Englishman, Richard Millinchamp; a Dane named Richard Johnson; and two Americans from Massachusetts, Aldin Chapin and Nathaniel Savory. All were sailors tired of the sea, deck hands who from now on wanted to look at the ocean across a wide beach rather than over the side of a ship. The ports of the Pacific were full of such men, and only accident brought these five together at Honolulu. Savory had left his ship after losing part of one hand in an accident with a saluting cannon in Honolulu harbor. Mozarro, whose checkered career included shipwreck on an uninhabited island in the Indian Ocean, arrived rather mysteriously at Honolulu in 1830 with a boatload of girls from the Marquesas Islands. The others were men of obscure past, and not much future as long as they continued to go to sea. They had nothing to lose and perhaps something to gain by settling a new island.

A British schooner dropped Mozarro and his company at Peel Island in June, 1830. The first year was very hard, but after a season or two it became clear that they could grow almost anything they wanted in the fertile soil around Port Lloyd—corn, sweet potatoes, yams, melons, beans, onions, taro, sugar cane, coconuts, bananas, even tobacco. They turned their hogs and goats loose in the hills and then hunted them with dogs. In the harbor at Port Lloyd lazed hundreds of gigantic turtles, so many that in season the shallow water was thick with them. The meat was

62

MRS. J. H. MAGRUDER, JR.

U.S. News and World Report

General Yosio Tachibana surrenders the islands to Commodore John H. Magruder, Jr., U.S.N., in September, 1945; and by permission of the Navy, displaced Bonin islanders now living in Japan visit their ancestors' graves on Chichi Jima in 1965.

delicious, either fresh or cured. (There were almost as many sharks as turtles in the harbor, and one astonished visitor mentioned seeing intrepid dogs run into the shallows and drag small sharks out by the fins.)

Mozarro and the others had brought with them fifteen Hawaiians, five men and ten women, to work their farms on a sharecropping basis. The scheme failed. In a very short time each settler withdrew to his own hut and truck garden with his one or two native "wives." Many of the Hawaiians left as soon as they could and had to be replaced by "Kanakas," lazy, indigent drifters from Hawaii and other Pacific islands. The women were disinclined to raise children, and some followed the old Hawaiian customs of abortion and infanticide. Shipwrecked sailors, deserters, mutineers, and sick and disabled seamen came ashore—more than sixty in the first seven years —but only a handful stayed, and very few of those were interested in hard work.

Life could be comfortable all the same. Aldin Chapin was well set up by 1836, so a visitor reported. In his square, one-room house stood "a table, covered with newspapers and writing materials, and over it, upon the wall, hung a spy glass, and a thin manuscript, headed 'Laws of the Bonin Isles.' A sea chest stood on each side of the room, and a bed, with calico curtains, filled each corner. A few French prints, and a shelf of fifty or sixty miscellaneous volumes, occupied rather than adorned the walls. A chair of home manufacture and a three legged stool completed the furniture."

Chapin was the most literate man at Port Lloyd, a natural keeper of the "laws." The settlers' code was simple enough, suitable to a colony where only three men (including Savory and Chapin but not Mozarro) could write their names. All disputes were supposed to be settled by majority vote. No one was to help sailors desert from ships, and no one was to "maltreat the slaves or servants of another, or endeavour to seduce any woman from her lord." Those who made their marks at the foot of this document in 1836 did so grudgingly, at the urging of a visiting American naval commander. A few years later another commander, this time a Britisher, called a meeting to discuss law and order, but his spokesman, the English settler Richard Millinchamp, "was assailed with the most violent oaths and the greatest abuse, which were accompanied with the threat of his life." No piece of paper would protect such men from each other or from themselves. Every so often Mozarro hoisted his Union Jack, and once he made a trip to Honolulu, returning with written confirmation of his leadership supplied by the acting British consul, but these were the emptiest of gestures.

Port Lloyd really had no law to stand between grievance and vengeance, and Mozarro was as ready as the next man to look for direct redress. Over the years he found Savory and Chapin on the opposite side in arguments far too often. He decided the colony would be better off without the disputatious Americans. His plan to rid himself of them backfired, and in 1838 Savory and Chapin got from one Francis Silver a remarkable document: "I . . . do make oath of the following: That Mr. Matthew Mozarro told me some time since that if he could get Chapin and Savory out of the way he would give everything he possessed in the world. . . . He said for me to . . . wait for Savory . . . and for me to go close alongside of him for to make friends with Savory and when he turns his head . . . to beat his Brains out with a club, and if that did not kill him to stab him with a knife until dead and throw him into the sea. I then answered that I would not do it. A few days after he told me he would give me some Laudanum and for me to give it to Savory's girl and for her to put it in Savory's tea and poison him."

Quite apart from the murderous fantasies of Mozarro, Savory and the other islanders had to contend with rioting seamen who came ashore from passing whalers. At Port Lloyd during the busy "Japan season" the settlers were powerless, forced to retreat to the hills while the whalemen cut a careless swath through the village, drinking, firing their guns, and pursuing the Kanaka women.

Yet Savory had something to gain from the whalers. An industrious New Englander, with commercial contacts at Honolulu and other ports in the Pacific, he had built up a fortune of a few thousand dollars selling rum and supplies on Peel Island. By the end of the eighteen forties he was easily the richest man at Port Lloyd. This meant that he also had a lot to lose. In 1849 a merchant captain named Barker put in for supplies and repairs, and stayed to loot the settlement. Savory and the others fled to the highlands. In the midst of Barker's attack, a French whaler arrived. Nine of her men jumped ship and joined the wreckers, and when their captain tried to get them back, Barker gave them weapons. Savory lost about two thousand dollars in cash and several thousand dollars' worth of provisions; the rioters emptied his house down to his diary. When Barker sailed in January, 1850, he took with him the French deserters and also two Kanakas, one of them Savory's girl, who apparently had led the sailors to her "lord's" cache of money.

Savory was almost back where he started. A less stubborn man might have quit the island, but Savory stayed. Within a few years he was the only one of the original white settlers left. Millinchamp and Johnson drifted away, and Chapin died. Savory's old enemy Mozarro had died in 1847, and in 1850 Savory married his widow, Maria, a handsome young woman from Guam. Showing more respect for form than was usual at Port Lloyd, he took Maria out beyond the three-mile limit in a Yankee whaler called *No Duty*

On Tea, and had the captain legally marry them. During the next few years he and his wife began to pick up the threads of a settled life again.

On the other side of the world, late in 1852, Commodore Perry's expedition was heading eastward. All the way across the Atlantic, Perry gave thought to the problem of combining his long-term plans for the Bonins and his immediate task of negotiating a treaty with the unapproachable government of Japan. "As a preliminary step, and one of easy accomplishment," he wrote to the Secretary of the Navy, "the squadron should establish places of rendezvous at one or two of the islands south of Japan, having a good harbor, and possessing facilities for obtaining water and supplies." Perry the great stage manager wanted, in fact, some sort of prepared base to which he could withdraw after making a first dazzling impression on the Japanese, and from which he would return in due course to consummate his treaty.

Two places came to mind—the town of Naha on the island of Okinawa in the Ryukyus, vaguely a dependency of Japan, and Port Lloyd on Peel Island, the only safe harbor in the Bonins. Perry decided to visit Okinawa first. With luck, he could learn something there about eastern diplomacy before the time came to commit himself in Japan, and in turn the Okinawans might send advance notice to the Japanese that Perry's black warships came in peace. It was one of those good ideas that did not work at all. For two weeks Perry and the governors of Okinawa indulged in a wary and absurd ritual dance of protocol, and then, with very little accomplished, Perry broke off negotiations and sailed for the Bonins.

The *Susquehanna* and the *Saratoga* were welcomed heartily at Port Lloyd when they arrived on June 14, 1853, and the squadron's surveyors, scientists, artists, and writers were able to go about their business on Peel Island free from the government surveillance that had plagued them at Okinawa. Perry himself found it unnecessary to stay aboard his flagship rejecting inept overtures from unsuitable envoys, as he had done at Naha. He went ashore, met Savory, and bought from him for fifty dollars a stretch of land one thousand yards by five hundred, close to Ten Fathom Hole, the anchorage at the north end of the harbor. This was the first piece of territory in the Far East to come under American control; Perry intended it to be used as a coaling station for American ships. In one day at the Bonins he had accomplished more than he had in two weeks at Okinawa. The reason was simple: here there was no government with which he had to negotiate; Savory was selling part of his private property, and Perry spoke to him as one New Englander to another.

CONTINUED ON PAGE 69

64

Our former Secretary of State recalls his service fifty years ago in the Connecticut National Guard—asthmatic horses, a ubiquitous major, and a memorable

range practice

By DEAN ACHESON

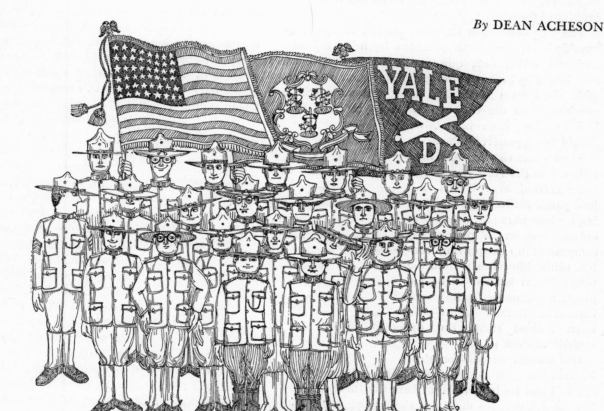

The calendar has it that these events occurred fifty years ago last summer. It is hardly more credible than that a thousand ages can be like an evening gone. But as President Lincoln said, "we cannot escape history." Nineteen sixteen was the year of the Wilhelmstrasse's amazingly successful plot to distract President Wilson's attention from the war in Europe by involving him with Mexico, of General "Black Jack" Pershing's invasion of Mexico in "hot pursuit" of Pancho Villa, after that worthy had staged a raid across the Rio Grande on Columbus, New Mexico. Poor General Pershing never caught up with Villa.

But President Wilson caught up with the realiza-

tion that the United States had no army. Improvising, he called out the National Guard and mustered it into the federal service. This is where I came in. Having finished the first year of law school and being without plans for the summer, I was easy prey for the press gang in the form of friends in the so-called Yale Battery, Battery D of the Connecticut National Guard's Regiment of Field Artillery. In no time I found myself that lowly form of military life, a private and "driver" in the old horse-drawn field artillery. Garbed in a hilariously ill-fitting uniform and Stetson hat with its red cord, I made my small contribution to the gloriously unorganized confusion of our journey from

65

ILLUSTRATED FOR AMERICAN HERITAGE BY RICHARD ROSENBLUM

New Haven to training camp at Tobyhanna in the Pocono hills of Pennsylvania.

None of our batteries had ever owned any horses. Those used in the evening drills in New Haven had been moonlighting, supplementing a more mundane daytime existence as brewery and dray horses. We would get our horses, so we were told, at Tobyhanna. They would come to us from the West—an interesting thought, this. Would we be, we wondered, the first bipeds they had ever seen? Our imagination was far inferior to the reality.

The first disillusion came on arrival. It was with mankind. We had been preceded by a New Jersey regiment which had, quite naturally, appropriated the best sites and everything movable. Our relations with them soon resembled those between colonial contingents in the Continental Army, meaning that had Hessians been handy, we should have preferred them.

Then came the horses. Those assigned to the New Jersey regiment arrived first. Words sink into pallid inadequacy. Our first impressions were gay: a vast panoramic cartoon of our enemy campmates in side-splitting trouble. Blithe horse-spirits from the Great Plains seemed to be enjoying a gymnastic festival, with inanimate human forms scattered around them. But the comedy was not to last.

Our horses emerged from their boxcars strangely docile. Only occasionally would an eye roll and heels fly or teeth bare in attempted mayhem or murder. No more was the landscape gay with mad scenes of separating centaurs. Over the whole camp a pall settled, broken only by asthmatic wheezes and horse coughs. Stable sergeants and veterinary officers hurried about with worried faces. The wretched horses had caught cold in the chill night mountain air, so different from that of their warm, free prairies. The colds had become pneumonia and contagious.

Then they began to die. One has no idea how large an animal a horse is until faced with the disposal of a dead one, and in the Poconos, where solid rock lies barely two feet under the surface! It was no illusion, to those whose picks drew only sparks, that the bodies of the deceased grew faster than their graves. Soon we were all pleading with the sufferers to be of good heart, not to give up the battle for life; we put slings under them to keep them on their feet; tenderly gave them the veterinarians' doses; manned round-the-clock watches at the stables.

At just this time, far off in the higher echelons of the Army, some keen leader of men decided to raise the morale of the troops by inspecting them. The choice fell on Major General Leonard Wood, late a physician and Teddy Roosevelt's C.O. in the Rough Riders, then commanding the Eastern Department of the Army and soon to be Governor General of the Philippines and a presidential aspirant. At that time not even Alexander the Great would have impressed us, much less imbued us with martial spirit. We were sunk too deep in the horse-undertaking business.

A friend was doing midnight-to-four sentry duty at our stables. Lanterns bobbed and boots slid on stone as a party approached. Tearing himself away from the nuances of horse breathing, he shouted "Halt! Who goes there?" Back came the ominous answer, "The Commanding General of the Eastern Department."

Rapidly exhausting his knowledge of military repartee, my friend ordered, "Advance to be recognized." General Wood stepped into the lamplight. The sentry did not know him from the mayor of Philadelphia, but the stars on his shoulders were enough, and, anyway, he had run out of small talk. He managed a snappy salute and the word "sir!" which seemed safe enough.

General Wood took over. His examination brought out that the sentry was guarding the battery's stable, or part of it, and that the stable was, not surprisingly, inhabited by horses. He then sought to probe the vaunted initiative of the American soldier. "What would you do," he asked, "if, while you were on duty, one of these horses was taken sick?" For a moment the enormity of this question flooded my friend's mind, submerging all consciousness of military protocol. When he could speak, the outrage of it burst through. "Jesus, General, they're *all* sick!" Like Bret Harte's Ah Sin, when the ace fell out of his sleeve in the poker game, "subsequent proceedings interested him no more."

At the height of the horse crisis I was ordered to report to the Captain's tent. General consensus recognized Captain Carroll Hincks as a good guy. A few years ahead of us at Yale, he had just begun to practice law in New Haven. He did his best to be a good soldier and a good battery commander. To say that his natural gifts lay in his own profession is no disparagement, since he was destined to become a highly respected federal judge, first on the district bench and later on the court of appeals.

The Captain began—truth forces me to admit—with a gross understatement, followed by an even grosser untruth. "You may be aware," he said, "of the dissatisfaction of the men with the food being served to them." Remembering the troubles of my friend at the stables, a simple "Yes, sir" seemed an adequate reply. To coin a phrase, the food was God-awful.

"Very well," he went on, "I'm going to give you a great opportunity." A clear lie, obviously. Captains did not give privates opportunities; they only gave them headaches. "You will be promoted to the rank of sergeant and put in charge of the mess."

A nice calculation of the evils before me would have required an advanced type of computer. In the descending circles of hell, horse-burial details were clearly lower than mess sergeants—closer to the central fire and suffering. Mess sergeants suffered only social obloquy. But redemption worked the other way. The horses might get well or all die. But those who became mess sergeants all hope abandoned. Corporals, even little corporals, might become emperors, but no mess sergeant ever got to be a shavetail. However, the Captain had not offered me a choice; he had pronounced a judgment. "Yes, sir," I said again, and was dismissed.

As things turned out, life proved tolerable. One help was that the food could not get worse; another, that one of the cooks was not without gifts which, when sober, he could be inspired to use. It only remained to convince the regimental sergeant major that after the cook's Bacchic lapses the true function of the guardhouse was to sober him up, not to reform him. All in all, things began to look up. Although the very nature of the soldier requires that he beef about his food, the beefing in Battery D began to take on almost benevolent profanity. That is, until the Major entered our lives.

In real life—if I may put it that way—the Major was a professor, a renowned archeologist and explorer of lost civilizations, obvious qualifications for supervising regimental nutrition and hygiene. He turned his attention first to food. The rice we boiled, he correctly pointed out, seemed to flow together, in an unappetizing starchy mass. In the Andes, he said, they prevented this by boiling the rice in paper bags. Aside from the inherent implausibility of this procedure, it seemed to have no relation to the end sought. But the professor-turned-Major showed no inclination to debate the point; and an order is an order according to the Articles of War. After all, it seemed to make little difference, since the bags, and even the hemp that tied them, simply disappeared into the gelatinous mass. But our customers found otherwise. They reported an indissoluble residue, impervious to chewing, soon identified as wood pulp. The Major was the killing frost that nipped the tender buds of the battery's good will toward me.

Then came the matter of the disposal of the dishwater in which the men washed their mess kits. Neither regulations nor regimental headquarters had considered, much less solved, this problem. However, we in the cookhouse had. We simply tipped the barrel over a small cliff behind the company street. No one criticized this eminently practical solution of a practical problem until the Major came along. He regarded it as unhygienic and again found the solution in Andean practice. There they had built fires within horseshoe-shaped, low stone walls and poured dishwater over the hot stones by the dipperful, turning it into a presumably sanitary steam. A ukase was issued to the kitchen police. Sullenly they built the stone  horseshoe and, after diligent scrounging for wood, the fire. Appalachian stone proved to be more heat resistant than the Andean variety. An hour's dipping hardly reduced the level of the dishwater and produced no steam. At this point the kitchen police, delivering a succinct statement of their view of the situation in general and of me specifically, poured the whole barrel of water over the fire, and signed off for the night. It was mutiny; but it was magnificent. Next morning, a new detail dumped the gruesome residue over the cliff. We resumed our former practice, leaving the stone horseshoe and a few charred logs as an outward and visible sign of the Major's diligent attention to hygiene.

Realizing that the reader, like a court, must not be wearied with cumulative proof, I mention only the deplorable incident of the Colonel's inspection and pass on. Lower officers did more than enough inspecting to maintain desirable standards. The Colonel's perusal was rare and was of purely ritualistic significance. No one, least of all himself, looked for or would call attention to defects, not because they weren't there, but because it would have been embarrassing. It would defeat the purpose of the ritual, just as it would for a visiting chief of state, reviewing a guard of honor, to point out a dusty shoe or a missing tunic button, or for the pope, being carried into St. Peter's, to tell a cardinal that he had his hat on backward.

The Major, however, lacked a sense of occasion. He seemed unaware that in ritual, form, not substance, is of the essence, that the officers attending the

Colonel were there as acolytes, not fingerprint experts. As the least of the acolytes, I joined the party at the mess hall and tagged along to the cookhouse. Everything shone. The cooks, sober and in clean aprons and hats, saluted. The Colonel returned their salute and murmured, "At ease," as he turned to go. The Major chose this moment to hook his riding crop under a large and shining tub hanging against the wall and pull it out a few inches. He might have been Moses striking the rock. A stream of unwashed dishes and pans poured out and bounced about. The group froze as the Colonel looked hard at the Major and then asked our captain and first lieutenant to see him at his quarters after the inspection. He walked on.

The first necessity was profanity. Little could be added to the already exhaustive analysis of the Major's failings. The shortcomings of the cooks and kitchen police hardly exceeded primitive stupidity. My own problems were not serious. Some sacrifice must be offered on the altar of discipline—passes curtailed, pay docked, and so on. But underlying opinion was clear. The real *faux pas* was the Major's, and the Colonel would see it that way—as he did.

Meanwhile the summer was passing. The horses' particular brand of pneumococcus seemed to lose its zest. As they recovered, they became more amenable to military discipline. Soon the drivers had the caissons rolling along; and the gunners grew proficient at mental arithmetic as they listened to the shouted numbers, twirled the wheels that moved their gun barrels, and learned to push home dummy shells, lock the breeches, and jump aside to avoid a theoretical recoil as lanyards were pulled.

South of the border the political temperature cooled as the days shortened. General Pershing came home empty-handed, rumors flew that the National Guard

would be demobilized; but not before we had had a day of range practice, not before the effort and sweat of summer had been put to the test of firing live ammunition. Labor Day came and went. The mountain foliage began to turn, the blueberries to ripen on the hillsides. A few trenches were dug on a hill across a valley, enemy battery emplacements were simulated with plywood, notices were posted to warn berry pickers off the range on the chosen day. The Major was posted as range officer to ride over the target area before firing began to ensure that it was clear.

On a glorious autumn morning the regiment set out for the firing position, a plateau some miles beyond our camp at the far end of the military reservation. On the parade ground the sight of the full regiment in formation was a moving one; but when Battery D brought up the end of the column of march and our rolling kitchen took its place at the end of that, martial spirit suffocated under a pall of dust. Not a breath of air moved it. Only a wet handkerchief over the nose and mouth kept lungs from filling solid.

A brief respite came when the column halted and the kitchens moved up from the tail to the head of the batteries. The drivers watered and fed their horses while the gunners ate and then took their place. Even though the Major was far away on his assigned range patrol, we risked no chances with that meal—no boiled rice—there was too much live ammunition around. Not long after lunch the column debouched onto the plateau and moved straight across it. As Battery D emerged, the column broke into a trot, then swung at right angle into regimental front with guidons fluttering. When they were aligned, a bugle sent the whole command into a full gallop, a brave sight. As they reached firing position, they swung around, unlimbered guns and caissons, and took the horses, still excited and tossing their heads, to the rear.

We left the kitchen to the drivers and joined a group at the steps to a platform from which the Colonel was observing the terrain through field glasses. The last preparations for firing had been completed, gun crews and officers were in their places, range finders manned. Soon officers shouted numbers as they computed distances, angles, and elevations; wheels on the guns turned. The regulation procedure from here on was pretty conventional. One or two guns would fire a long and then a short—that is, on the first they would add to the estimated range, on the second, subtract. Having thus, hopefully, bracketed the target, they would split the difference, or make other correction, and everyone would be ready for business.

The Colonel turned to his second-in-command. "Range clear?" he asked with rising inflection. The words were repeated across the platform and down the steps. The words were picked up and rolled back as a receding breaker is by an incoming one. This time the inflection was reversed, assertive; not a question but an answer, "Range clear!" Then from the platform came the electrifying command: "Regimental salvo!"

The usual procedure might be conventional, but the Colonel was not. He would start this exercise with a bang that few present would forget. In sixteen guns shells were shoved home, breeches slammed shut; gunners jumped clear while lanyard sergeants watched for the signal. "Fire!" said the Colonel. The resultant roar was eminently satisfactory. Some of the horses snorted and gave a plunge or two. The whole hilltop across the valley burst into smoke and dust.

About a mile our side of it appeared a separate source of dust bursts, moving toward us at great speed, touching, so it seemed, only the higher mounds. An order to cease fire stopped the reloading, and field glasses centered on the speeding horseman. Word spread that it was the forgotten Major. As he came nearer, he seemed to be urging the horse to greater effort. Panic or rage or both had clearly taken over.

He would certainly gallop up flushed and breathing hard, fling himself from the saddle, and run toward the steps shouting, "What damned fool . . . ?" One could see him, stopped by the Colonel's cold stare, salute and stammer out, "Range clear, sir!" I didn't wait for the confrontation. The platform would soon be the scene of high words, possibly controversy, in any event, unpleasantness. It was clearly no place for a mess sergeant who belonged with his field kitchen.

For a few days much talk and questioning revolved about who said what to whom. Unfortunately I could not help with this since I had rejoined the kitchen group before the dialogue began and was quite as puzzled as the others about what had happened. Anyway, it was all forgotten in a few days when we broke camp for the move home and mustering out.

Years later I met the Major again. We had both exchanged military titles for somewhat higher civilian ones. But although we were to see a good deal of one another, not always under the pleasantest circumstances, it never seemed to me that our relationship would be improved by probing the events of that memorable range practice.

The Bonins–Isles of Contention CONTINUED FROM PAGE 64

Savory had now been on the beach for twenty-three years, but he still carried his American seaman's papers. Perry attached him to the squadron as a temporary crew member, appointed him resident U.S. agent at Port Lloyd, and left a seaman to help look after the purchase at Ten Fathom Hole. As some of his predecessors had done, Perry tried his hand at making a constitution for Port Lloyd. With his encouragement a document entitled "Articles of Agreement of the Settlers of Peel Island" was drawn up, and Savory was elected chief magistrate.

Perry stayed only four days at the Bonins, but this was long enough to convince him that his interest was well founded. Later in 1853 one of his ships claimed the uninhabited southern cluster for the United States, and just before he left on his voyage home, Perry sent the settlers at Peel Island an American flag. "It is to be hoped," he wrote to Savory, "that steps may ere long be taken to give greater importance to Port Lloyd."

While he was in the Far East, Perry exchanged some sharp letters with J. G. Bonham, British superintendent for trade at Hong Kong, over the sovereignty of the Bonins. The correspondence ended on a note of compromise, with Perry saying that he would be quite happy to see a free port at Peel Island if the two home governments would agree to such a solution.

But they did nothing. When next a sovereign nation took an interest in the Bonins it was Japan. In 1859 the islands were scouted for the Japanese whaling industry by that remarkable man Nakahama Manjiro, who knew more at first hand about the English-speaking world than any other Japanese (see "The Man Who Discovered America" in the December, 1956, AMERICAN HERITAGE). Nakahama had already been of great service to his country during Perry's visit, and in 1860–61 he was a member of the first Japanese embassy to the United States. He and the other envoys carried home with them several copies of the published reports of Perry's expedition, and the Commodore's ambitious plans for the Bonins were immediately noted. It was enough to convince the Japanese government that action was needed.

The strategy developed by the shogunate was Perry's own, reflected in a mirror of Japanese design. The instrument of annexation must be an imposing naval expedition backed by armed force. The infant Japanese Navy had nothing to match Perry's black ships, but eventually the *Kanrin Maru,* built to Japanese orders by the Dutch in 1856 and fresh from an overhaul after taking the embassy to America in 1860, was readied for the task. The *Kanrin Maru* anchored at Port Lloyd on January 17, 1862; a shore party planted the Japanese flag on a thousand-foot hill behind the harbor and named the peak Asahi Yama, "Mountain of the Rising Sun."

The first government official to land asked the settlers, "Have you people come here by command of some sovereign?" The answer of course was No, and this was the cue for the senior negotiator to make his appearance. Mizuno Chikugo no Kami Tadanori came ashore, arrayed in ceremonial robes of office and wearing the double swords of the samurai. Mizuno's translator was Nakahama Manjiro.

Mizuno did Savory the courtesy of interviewing him in a purple tent, the color of high rank, and addressing him as a person of samurai status, but he was politely contemptuous of all Western claims to the islands, saying that a famous Japanese of the sixteenth century, Ogasawara Sadayori, had discovered and explored the chain, and that consequently priority rights belonged to Japan. The story of Ogasawara was a complete fiction, but it had enjoyed a long and sturdy life in Japan, and Mizuno and his fellow officials knew from its inclusion in Perry's reports that it was given some credence in the West.

With a minimum of disturbance, Mizuno persuaded Savory and the other islanders to acknowledge Japan's control. The names given to the islands in 1675 were resurrected; Peel Island became Chichi Jima once more, and Port Lloyd was given the name of Futami-Ko. New harbor regulations were drawn up, the settlers' lands were surveyed and their titles confirmed, the island's currency was stabilized (in Mexican dollars, which were common in the Pacific), and hunting and wood cutting in the hills were controlled. On Mizuno's return to Tokyo, his government, overriding all foreign diplomatic objections, announced that the Bonins were indisputably Japanese.

The first shipload of Japanese colonists, recruited in the Izus, arrived at Futami-Ko in September, 1862. For them, good land was hard to find. Savory and the others had long since staked out the best plots, and the newcomers under Governor Obana Sakunosuke had to work hard to set their village, which was named Omura, on the way to self-sufficiency. The white settlers, their Hawaiian wives, and their mixed offspring lived mostly around Ten Fathom Hole. The two groups did not see much of each other; whenever business had to be transacted, Savory and Obana acted as go-betweens.

Before the Japanese colonists were fairly on their feet they were hit by a political upheaval in Japan

Some hint of Perry's rather overwhelming effect upon the Japanese is seen in this portrait sketched by a native artist.

70

that reversed the national policy of expansion, bringing back the introversion of earlier days. In June, 1863, a Japanese ship appeared carrying orders for Obana: the colony was to be dismantled and the colonists sent home. In less than a week they were gone. Obana left Savory in charge of the property that remained, with the express warning that this abrupt departure did not mean that Japan was surrendering her sovereignty.

By the end of the eighteen sixties Savory was seventy-five years old, but he was still not old enough to sit quietly and watch an aggressive interloper take over the Bonins. The Japanese government was one thing; Captain Benjamin Pease was quite another. Pease, in the words of an indignant man who knew him well, was a "villian of the first water." He claimed to be an American and was a trafficker in the dubious labor trade of the Pacific, picking up and delivering shiploads of willing or unwilling Kanakas to plantation owners. He took up residence at Port Lloyd in 1871 and went into business as a planter and trader.

Soon he was calling himself "Governor" Pease. In 1873 he visited the United States minister at Tokyo to ask what protection Americans in business at the Bonins might expect from their home government. Given sufficient inducement, Pease explained, he might be persuaded to remain at the islands and accept a United States consulship. The minister made inquiries and received a less than enthusiastic letter from Washington on the general subject of Americans in far places, and the matter of "Consul" Pease ended there. But his fame spread across the Pacific to San Francisco, where it was reported that he had taken

full possession of Peel Island, was flying the Stars and Stripes, and was ready to sell to the United States.

At Port Lloyd, Pease crossed swords with Nathaniel Savory and his grown sons. They argued about the ownership of a consignment of whale oil and about the death of some sheep, and then they argued about their arguments. It had all the makings of a feud, with Pease announcing at last that Savory had issued an "open Chalange which I readily accept and let the bitter end come as soon as it likes." One of Savory's friends heard Pease say "that if you [Savory] did not let him alone and quit talking about him he was going to the cove and hang you to your door post."

Savory died in April, 1874—a natural death. Pease was murdered about six months later. His wife (a part-white girl named Susan Robinson, survivor of an earlier mass murder on Haha Jima, in the southern cluster) had caught the eye of a Negro named Spenser, who worked for Pease. One day in October, 1874, Pease took a canoe round the coast, and soon afterward it was found bottom up and stove in on the shore. There was no sign of Pease. Spenser lived just long enough for Susan Pease to bear him a child. Then he too went out in a canoe and never came back. The canoe was found, and in it was Spenser's coat, torn by a turtle hook and soaked in blood.

The United States minister at Tokyo interested himself for a short time in these disappearances, but they were never fully explained. The minister did find that Pease's citizenship, like everything else about him, was dubious. He might have been an American, but then again he might not. In any case he was gone. Since 1830 eleven people (counting Pease and Spenser) had been murdered at the Bonins, quite a high figure for a settlement that never numbered more than a few score adults. There was no law at Port Lloyd, no religion, only a pretense at marriage between white men and native women, and no education for the children. One or two men like Nathaniel Savory and Thomas Webb had tried to keep self-respect alive, but a good many others who found their way to the islands were not much better than animals. After four and a half decades of occupation by Europeans, the Bonins fitted all too well Perry's disdainful description of a primitive Pacific island—unproductive, mismanaged by savages, doomed to be swallowed up by a more efficient race.

In 1875 the Japanese returned. The shogunate had been overthrown and the imperial government restored in 1868, and a climate favorable to expansion had again developed. By the mid-1870's the government was ready to act. Foreign Minister Terashima Munenori stated his country's new policy on the Bonins: they were of historic interest, they had been colonized in the eighteen sixties, and besides, in the "golden words of an ancient sage," to "abandon islands in neighboring waters is bad for a country."

The official party that came to Port Lloyd aboard the *Meiji Maru* in November, 1875, found the Stars and Stripes flying there. It had been Nathaniel Savory's dying wish that the American flag should be shown whenever a ship came into the harbor, and his widow faithfully carried out his request. His son, Horace Perry Savory, whose middle name was a reminder of the Great Commodore's visit, led the settlers in signing away their independence, this time permanently. In 1876 the Bonins, renamed Ogasawara Gunto after the legendary discoverer, became the responsibility of the Japanese Ministry of Home Affairs.

Japan was on the brink of several decades of expansion in the Pacific. She took the Kuriles as well as the Bonins in 1875, the Ryukyus in 1879, Formosa and the Pescadores in 1895, southern Sakhalin in 1905, and was given mandates over the Marianas, the Carolines, and the Marshalls after World War I. In the Western Pacific, Perry's "more efficient race" was clearly the Japanese.

New colonists, most of them from the Izus, came to the Bonins in increasing numbers, to settle on Chichi Jima and Haha Jima. The seat of government at Futami-Ko, the old Port Lloyd, acquired a police station, a courthouse, a school, a post office, a Shinto shrine, and a monument to Ogasawara, whose mythical exploits were remembered by an annual holiday.

For a time it appeared as if the little group of Bonin islanders living around Ten Fathom Hole (in a village with the new name of Okumura) would simply be swallowed up. In 1876 only one of them was literate—the Englishman, Webb—and they had few institutions to hold them together. One by one they swore allegiance to Japan, and by 1882 all were naturalized citizens.

In Nathaniel Savory's time the settlers had never farmed more than a hundred and fifty acres around Port Lloyd. The Japanese attacked the land enthusiastically, clearing hundreds of acres more. They experimented with many crops, including coffee and rubber, and finally determined that the sugar cane, vegetables, and tropical fruits raised there could be sold profitably in the home islands of Japan.

The Japanese whaling and fishing fleets used Futami-Ko in season. Late in the nineteenth century they were joined by American sealers, who pursued the migrating herds along the Japan Current and slaughtered seals by thousands with shotguns.

Aboard a typical sealer named the *Sophie Sutherland* an untypical seventeen-year-old named Jack London came to Futami-Ko in 1893. He was just discovering in himself an ambition to be a writer, and when he went back to San Francisco after a season among the seal herds, he put his experiences on paper. All day long at Futami-Ko, he recalled, the crack-shot seal hunters stalked boars and steers in the hills; then they gathered at the harbor to drink the night away. London was not yet an accomplished drinker. He was tipsy enough early one evening to engage a Japanese orchestra at a "house of entertainment"; later he fell asleep in the doorway of the port pilot's home, waking up to find his watch, money, coat, belt, and shoes gone. The stronger heads drank on.

As well as picking up supplies and letting off steam at Futami-Ko, the Americans recruited seal hunters, finding the best of these among the descendants of the old settlers living around Nathaniel Savory's land at the village of Okumura, or Yankeetown, as its residents persisted in calling it. In the veins of the Savorys, Webbs, Gilleys, Washingtons, Robinsons, and Gonzaleses flowed the mingled blood of Americans, Englishmen, Germans, West Indian Negroes, Hawaiians, Guamanians, and other Pacific islanders. They all shared a taste for the sea. They could handle small craft expertly, and in time they developed modified outrigger canoes and whaleboats that amazed the Japanese with their speed and seaworthiness. Most men of Yankeetown could not see the point of grubbing around in the earth for food when there were fish to be caught and seals to be shot.

Surrounded by farmers from Japan, the seagoing descendants of the old settlers cultivated their sense of separateness. A good many of them became members of an Anglican missionary church where English was spoken, and were married there to mates chosen from within their own group. Some of the younger generation, however, married Japanese, and by the 1920's the Yankeetown people were less than a hundred in a population of several thousand. But nothing could persuade them to surrender their identity. They looked different, they thought differently, they *were* different, no matter what their citizenship papers said.

By the 1920's the Pacific, that "immense ocean" of which Commodore Perry spoke, had become crowded. Japan's successes on the Asian continent and in the islands during World War I led her to think in terms of an Asian Monroe Doctrine. After the war a conference was held at Washington to encourage interested parties to reconcile their oceanic ambitions. One of the main issues dividing the United States and Japan was the question of naval bases in the Pacific islands. The Japanese delegates made a strong bid to have the Bonins recognized as an integral part of Japan, because this would allow them to fortify the harbor at Futami-Ko without restriction. Anticipating heavy opposition, the Japanese armed forces had done considerable work in the Bonins before the conference opened. After some hard bargaining, Japan lost the decision: Article XIX of the Five Power Treaty stipulated that the military status quo should be preserved in several groups of islands, including the Bonins. Japan chose not to obey the prohibition. Only a few years later the emperor visited Chichi Jima to watch his Navy carry out war games there, and by that time the Bonins were under martial law. Foreigners found it more and more difficult to gain access to the islands, and at last, in 1935, even the Anglican missionary bishop whose flock included the tiny congregation at Yankeetown was barred.

When war came in 1941, Chichi Jima was one of a string of island fortresses stretching south from the Izus through the Bonins to the Volcanoes (where Iwo Jima was the strategic center) and on to Saipan and Tinian in the Japanese-mandated Marianas. At Futami-Ko the anchorage had been dredged to accommodate everything from seaplanes and submarines to battleships, and the hills behind the harbor had been blasted and drilled to make air-conditioned, copper-lined, bomb-proof caves for storing ammunition.

In the first years of the war, Chichi Jima's role was simply to supply Japan's forward bases to the south. Not until the tide turned in favor of the Allies

The rather pleasant life available on the Bonins at the time of Perry's visit in 1853 was suggested in engravings made for his Narrative of the Expedition of an American Squadron to the China Seas and Japan, *from sketches made by his artists. Left: "Natural Tunnel, Port Lloyd"—on Peel Island, the main island of the group. Right, in sequence: "South East Bay," on the same island—evidently a good spot for swimming; "Valley Near South East Bay"; and "Stapleton Island" —the northernmost island, and obviously good hunting ground.*

in the Pacific did the island come under attack by bombers on their way to and from the Japanese home islands. Late in 1943 the strategic thinking of the Allies became organized around the idea of a Pacific triangle, with Tokyo at the apex. As the leapfrogging island war went on, the sides of the triangle were shortened, and advanced bomber bases were planned —Okinawa in the west, and the most suitable island along "the ladder of the Bonins" in the east. But Iwo Jima in the Volcanoes was chosen over Chichi Jima, first because its terrain was less rugged and bomber airstrips could be built there more easily, and second because intelligence reports showed that the fortress of Chichi Jima would be even more difficult to take than Iwo Jima.

Once American planes were able to use the airstrips on Iwo Jima, Chichi Jima, only a hundred and fifty miles to the north, was bombed every day for weeks. All civilians had been evacuated in the summer of 1944, including the people of Yankeetown, who were assigned Japanese names and sent to Tokyo and Yokohama. The garrison at Futami-Ko spent most of its time in the caves behind the harbor. There were no Japanese war heroes in the Bonins. During the last months of the war the Allies bypassed Chichi Jima, and in September, 1945, Lieutenant General Yosio Tachibana surrendered to Commodore John H. Magruder, Jr., aboard the destroyer *Dunlap* off Futami-Ko.

American troops under Marine Colonel Presley M. Rixey arrived in October to begin the repatriation of Japanese soldiers, and in the tedious days that followed, victors and vanquished played baseball on the scarred small-plane airstrip. With Rixey came Fred Savory, great grandson of Nathaniel, to work as an interpreter. One of Rixey's tasks was to find out what had happened to several American flyers shot down over the Bonins. Savory and other islanders had heard gruesome rumors in Japan during the last months of the war. General Tachibana insisted that some of the prisoners had been sent to Japan and that the others

had lost their lives during American air raids, but Rixey, prompted by Savory, investigated further. His findings were that Tachibana and some of his subordinates had ordered the pilots executed by bayoneting and decapitation; that two of the bodies had been dismembered, and that Major Matoba Sueo served human flesh in his officers' mess. Nothing in modern international law prescribed a penalty for ritual cannibalism, but the penalty for murder was death. Tachibana, Matoba, and three other officers were hanged in 1947 after a war-crimes trial on Guam.

Under the terms of the Allies' Cairo Declaration of 1943, Japan, once defeated, was to be stripped of all Pacific islands seized or occupied by her since World War I. The Potsdam Declaration of 1945 limited Japanese sovereignty to the home islands, leaving the fate of the outliers to be determined later. After the war the United States Navy was given the responsibility of administering the Bonins and the Volcanoes, as well as the islands of the former Japanese mandate in Micronesia.

The Navy simply designated the Bonins a closed area. No plans were made to bring back the seven thousand Japanese civilians who had lived on Chichi Jima and Haha Jima before the war. But what would happen to the islanders from Yankeetown? Fred Savory drafted a petition to the State-War-Navy Coordinating Committee in Washington, asking that they be allowed to go home. The Navy approved, arguing that the islanders had been at Chichi Jima for generations, whereas most of the Japanese civilians were recent immigrants, supported only by military expenditure. The Yankeetown settlers deserved special consideration. Their western blood had left them open to persecution in Japan during the war, and several of them had been useful to the Allies after the war, helping to convict Japanese war criminals. They were an easily identifiable special group, and their numbers did not pose serious problems. In October, 1946, about one hundred and thirty islanders returned to

Chichi Jima, and Colonel Rixey flew the Stars and Stripes to welcome them.

The islanders were given Navy quonset huts to live in, and under the friendly eye of the Americans, the Savorys and their companions took up their interrupted life where they had left off in 1944. They regarded the islands and the coastal waters as theirs once more. Japanese boats venturing inside the three mile limit were likely to be fired at, and once the islanders shot and killed a poaching fisherman.

Soon after the end of the war the Japanese government began agitating for the return of their civilians to the Bonins. The Japanese-American treaty of 1952 allowed Japan "residual sovereignty" in all the southern islands, but left them under American administration. On Okinawa, the presence of a large American military force did not entail the permanent exclusion of Japanese civilians, but in the Navy's view American strategy in the Far East would be best served if the Bonins were empty of Japanese. Some men in the American State Department looked forward to the return of civilians to the Bonins, however, and when Robert Murphy was appointed United States Ambassador to Japan he intended to see that this was done "without delay." But Admiral Arthur W. Radford, Commander in Chief in the Pacific, changed Murphy's mind by taking him on a cruiser tour of the Bonins and explaining their strategic importance.

At the beginning of the 1950's the Navy was represented at the Bonins by a lone chief petty officer, who was assigned to help the Yankeetown fishermen put their port back in some kind of working condition. Year by year, however, the Navy increased its strength, creating by the end of the decade a top-secret base of unknown but obviously formidable capacity.

The Japanese government and the active League of Bonin Evacuees for Hastening Repatriation looked uneasily at this development. They argued along two lines: complete sovereignty over the Bonins should be returned to Japan, and expatriated civilians should be allowed to go back to the Bonins. Most of the League's members had suffered economic hardship by being separated from their lands, and in October, 1955, they sent a delegation to Washington to press their case. They were countered a month later by four men from Yankeetown (two of them named Savory), who were flown by Navy plane to the American capital: *they* petitioned, unsuccessfully, for the annexation of the Bonins by the United States and the grant of American citizenship to the islanders. In their minds the worst possible thing that could happen would be a new wave of Japanese immigration. As old Wilson Savory put it later, the islanders would be forced onto the beach "to eat coral dust."

The Japanese, temporarily setting aside the idea of civilian repatriation, turned to that of compensation. If dispossessed farmers could not go back to their lands in the Bonins, then at least they should be paid for the losses they had incurred. Twelve million dollars seemed to them a fair figure. In 1960 the United States Congress authorized the distribution of six and a half million dollars, and this somewhat mollified Japanese complaints about the American occupation.

In the early 1960's the Navy continued to regard the base at Chichi Jima as essential to American strategy in the Far East. By then the establishment in the Bonins included Navy men's wives and families, and American children on Chichi Jima were attending the Admiral Arthur Radford School. In the generation since the war, the islanders of Yankeetown had increased in number by about a hundred, and their children too went to Radford School. The islanders were still Japanese nationals, and most young men looked for brides in Japan. But their children were learning English, not Japanese; they saluted the American flag and recited the Pledge of Allegiance at school; and most of their parents hoped that American citizenship ultimately could be arranged for them.

But it seems more and more likely, as time passes, that the Bonins are going back to the Japanese government and to their thousands of displaced settlers. In mid-November, 1967, Premier Eisaku Sato came to Washington to see President Johnson—looking, he said, for something to put in the ten-gallon hat the President had given him on an earlier visit. One thing he got was an agreement that "the mutual security interests of Japan and the United States could be accommodated within arrangements for the return of administration of these islands [the Bonins] to Japan." Consultations to arrange the return are currently in progress.

Meanwhile, a few Japanese civilians have periodically been allowed to come to Chichi Jima to visit the graves of their war dead. The "American" islanders have taken no part in the observances, but have watched with mixed feelings as the visitors quietly repaired broken tombstones, said their prayers for the dead, and then departed, taking home to Japan handfuls of the rich soil that Commodore Perry had praised and Nathaniel Savory had plowed.

Gavan Daws teaches at the University of Hawaii and has just completed a history of Hawaii; Timothy Head, also a history teacher, recently returned from an assignment in Japan which enabled him to pursue that end of the research on the Bonins. Together they wrote an article about the island of Niihau for our October, 1963, issue.

The Great Red Scare

CONTINUED FROM PAGE 27

a "Bolshie coddler," took up the Secretary's main duties, while Abercrombie assumed control of immigration. On December 29, Abercrombie consented to a change in Rule 22 of the deportation-hearing procedure so that it no longer required the arresting officers to inform aliens of either their right to counsel or the charges against them. Two days later he issued some 3,000 mimeographed warrants for the arrest of aliens whose names were to be entered in the blanks.

The night of January 2 was chosen for a new set of raids. Agents who had infiltrated Communist cells were asked to arrange meetings for that evening "to facilitate arrests." The others were instructed to bring in as many aliens as they could find. Their orders, issued over the signature of Frank Burke, the assistant director of the Bureau of Investigation, said, in part, "I leave it entirely to your discretion as to the method by which you gain access to such places [where aliens might be].... If, due to local conditions in your territory, you find that it is absolutely necessary to obtain a search warrant for the premises, you should communicate with the local authorities a few hours before the time for the arrests is set." Otherwise plans for the raids were to be kept secret. The aliens were to be held incommunicado, and the agents were urged to secure "confessions" as quickly as possible.

The all-out raid went off on schedule in thirty-three cities in twenty-three states. Palmer's men were joined by local police, and in a few instances, though Palmer had earlier refused their help, by volunteer members of patriotic societies like the National Security League. By midnight of January 2 they had collected well over 3,000 suspects from the eastern industrial states, and from California, Washington, and Oregon in the West. The true number will never be known, for the records of that evening are hopelessly confused and in some areas nonexistent. All 3,000 mimeographed warrants were used—the names in many instances being added after the arrests were made—and an estimated 2,000 other suspects were picked up and held for some time without being charged.

Whatever the number, the results were spectacular. Editorial pages swiftly echoed the praises of public officials, and Palmer's reputation was at an all-time high. The effect of the raids, said the *New York Times,* should be "far-reaching and beneficial." Even the Washington *Post,* which had called the November arrests "a serious mistake," urged that the deportation of the new suspects take place as speedily as possible. "There is no time to waste," it said, "on hairsplitting over infringement of liberty." The Philadelphia *Inquirer* ran a jovial headline: ALL ABOARD FOR THE NEXT SOVIET ARK.

It was not, however, to be all that easy. After the initial enthusiasm had died down, and as complaints of wanton disregard of the aliens' civil rights found their way into print, a number of people began to question whether Palmer had not done more harm than good. The National Council of Churches started an investigation of the events of January 2. So did the Department of Labor. In Detroit a group of businessmen that included dime-store magnate S. S. Kresge looked into the raids that had taken place in that vicinity. Elsewhere other organizations did the same.

Their combined evidence revealed some shocking particulars. One man in Newark had been apprehended simply because—as the arresting officer put it —he "looked like a radical." Boston agents with drawn pistols had broken into the bedroom of a sleeping woman at 6 A.M. and dragged her off to headquarters without a warrant, only to find that she was an American citizen with no Communist connections. Attracted by the commotion on East Fifteenth Street, where the Russian People's House had again been raided, a New Yorker questioned a policeman about what was going on and shortly found himself on his way to jail. Police in Detroit arrested every diner in one foreign restaurant, and jailed an entire orchestra. Philadelphia agents booked a choral society en masse, and in Hartford, Connecticut, sympathetic aliens who were inquiring about some imprisoned friends were themselves held as suspects for nearly a week. Of 142 persons arrested in Buffalo, thirty-one turned out to be cases of "mistaken identity." In Detroit, where nearly eight hundred were arrested, less than four hundred warrants were served; four hundred and fifty warrants arrived to cover the other suspects two weeks after the raids had taken place.

Treatment of the aliens after the roundups was in many cases harsh. Four hundred men rounded up in New England were jammed into an underheated and overcrowded prison on Deer Island in Boston Harbor; there, in the next few weeks, one of them went insane, another jumped to his death from the fifth floor of the main cell block, and several others attempted suicide. When they were finally released, as most of them were, many were ill and a number showed signs of beatings. In Detroit, eight hundred suspects were lodged in a corridor of the United States Post Office building, without exterior ventilation, beds, or blankets. No food was distributed for twenty-four hours, and there was one toilet for the entire group. After two days of questioning, 340 of them were released, but over a hundred were imprisoned for more than a week in a detention cell 24 by 30 feet in the basement of the Municipal Building, where they lived on coffee and biscuits.

But the investigating committees discovered more than just dramatic instances of physical mistreatment. Twelve nationally known lawyers, including the Harvard Law School's Felix Frankfurter, Roscoe Pound, and Zechariah Chafee, Jr., issued at the end of May "A Report on the Illegal Practices of the United States Department of Justice." It was a sweeping indictment, solidly supported by evidence, of Palmer and his raids.

The real danger to the country, the lawyers wrote, lay not in the possibility of Red revolution, but in Palmer's obvious misuse of federal power. The Department of Justice, they said, had ignored due process of law in favor of "illegal acts," "wholesale arrests," and "wanton violence." Although the Fourth Amendment to the Constitution protects against arrest without prior warrant, Palmer's men had obtained only 3,000 writs for the more than 5,000 aliens eventually detained. Most of the warrants were defective, in any case; either they lacked substantiating proof, or they were unsworn and unsigned. All too frequently, they were unserved as well. "Instead of showing me a warrant," one suspect complained, "they showed me a gun." In the majority of cases, the federal agents carried no search warrants, either.

The twelve lawyers charged in their report that the raiders had violated the Fifth Amendment by making use of illegally obtained or hearsay evidence, or by resorting to dubious or fraudulent proof. At least two of the accused, for example, were held to be radicals on the grounds that they had been photographed reading Russian-language newspapers. Tickets to Socialist and Communist social functions, magazine subscription lists, post cards and letters from avowed Communists, and group photographs were introduced by the agents as acceptable evidence that suspected aliens belonged to revolutionary organizations. A New Jersey man was held because agents found plans for "an infernal machine" in his home; the mysterious drawings turned out to be blueprints for a phonograph. One agent turned in a stack of mock rifles from a dramatic society's prop room, but these and three .22 caliber target pistols were the only firearms Palmer's men found in any of the raids.

The lawyers' report went on to cite violations of the Sixth and Eighth Amendments. In many cases, counsel had been denied; no witnesses had been produced; interpreters had not been provided though few of the prisoners spoke fluent English; confessions had been obtained under the "third degree"; and

Life, July 3, 1919; CULVER PICTURES

The public pressure that drove Palmer to act against Russian aliens is suggested by this sardonic cartoon of 1919: "the law" threatens a Red bomber with "a slap on the wrist."

bail had often been set at an excessively high figure.

Palmer at first refused to concede that any of this was true. But as the evidence mounted, he finally admitted that "some" illegal acts might have taken place. "Trying to protect the community against moral rats," he declared some time afterward, "you sometimes get to thinking more of your trap's effectiveness than of its lawful construction." Hearing this, Louis Post ruefully noted that whatever Palmer might think, "the traps had been wretchedly put together." Judge George W. Anderson of the district court in Boston added, "A mob is a mob, whether made up of government officials acting under the instructions of the Justice Department, or of criminals and loafers."

By the spring of 1920, Palmer's anti-Red crusade was beginning to fall apart. In March, Abercrombie left the Department of Labor, and Post took his place. He immediately cancelled 2,000 of the original warrants as defective, and with the assistance of federal judges like Anderson, expedited hearings for those prisoners who remained in custody. Although Palmer had predicted that 2,720 aliens from the January raids would be deported, in the end only 556 were. In all, more than 4,000 suspects were released.

Shattered, the Attorney General urged Congress to impeach Post as a Communist sympathizer whose failure to press for convictions had let many dangerous radicals go free. After a month-long hearing, Post was found innocent and returned to his duties. Two months later, in June, Palmer himself was called before the House to answer charges that he had misused his office. The hearings ended inconclusively, but the charges were revived by the Senate Judiciary Committee the following year.

In a stormy committee session that began in January, 1921, Palmer stubbornly defended what his men had done. "I apologize for nothing," he told the committee. "I glory in it. I point with pride and enthusiasm to the results of that work. . . . [If my agents] were a little rough and unkind, or short and curt, with these alien agitators . . . I think it might well be overlooked in the general good to the country which has come from it."

By the time Palmer made his final statements on the raids, he was finished politically. He had flatly predicted a Communist uprising in May, 1920, and again on the Fourth of July. At first the press took him seriously, but when nothing happened the papers took to greeting his remarks with derision instead of alarm. For many people that summer, the Fighting Quaker had become a Don Quixote attacking an enemy that did not exist.

But he made one last, bold effort. In February, 1920, he had announced his candidacy for the Democratic presidential nomination, and when the convention opened in San Francisco late in June he had considerable support from the party regulars who remembered his long years of faithful service and who had benefited from his use of patronage when it was his to give. Others in the party, however, gravely doubted his ability to win, especially in the cities. It was clear to all that he had now lost the labor vote (one union magazine accused him of having used "the mailed fist of the autocratic tyrant"), and his own failure to define his stand on the League and on Prohibition worked against him. When the balloting began on July 2, he held the lead over his closest rival, William G. McAdoo, Wilson's Secretary of the Treasury and son-in-law, but he failed to get a majority. Thirty-seven ballots later, Palmer conceded the nomination, released the delegates who still supported him, and retired as the convention nominated Ohio's governor, James M. Cox.

His presidential dreams were over, and so was the Red Scare. Had the raids of January not fallen into disrepute by June, Palmer might have gone on to win in San Francisco. As it was, he returned to Washington a beaten man, and when he left the Cabinet in the spring of 1921, his departure was almost unnoticed by the papers that only a year before had bannered his name in their headlines. With the advent of the new administration, the Senate committee that was still investigating Palmer's work ended its deliberations; when its report was finally published two years later, no one much cared that the committee had passed no judgments but had merely offered a transcript of the testimony it had heard.

By then a general calm had settled on the nation and the world. Europe was rebuilding. Lenin had pulled back from his program of immediate world revolution and was turning his Russian people toward the quasi-capitalism of the New Economic Policy. The American economy was slowly coming back to normal, and management and labor had achieved a temporary peace. The press, which had done much to keep the public alerted to the activities of the domestic Reds, had found other topics to pursue.

There were still to be anti-Communist crusades in the years ahead, and the anti-alien sentiments that had led to the Palmer raids in the first place found expression in restrictive immigration laws and in the public uproar during the Sacco-Vanzetti trial. But most Americans were content to feel that the crisis had passed, if indeed there had been a crisis at all. In 1924 J. Edgar Hoover moved on to become the first (and thus far, only) director of the F.B.I. and periodically issued warnings that a Red threat was abroad in the land, but he never again resorted to the slap-dash techniques that he and his associates had developed in the days of the G.I.D.

In 1922 Palmer suffered the first of several heart attacks and retired from the political scene. A decade later, in an act that some have construed as making amends, he returned briefly to draft a Democratic program of moderate reform that served as one basis for F.D.R.'s New Deal campaign. Four years later, A. Mitchell Palmer was dead.

His old associates in government gathered for his funeral and paid homage for the progressive role he had played in his congressional days. But the nation as a whole remembered him only as the man they had goaded into a series of discredited raids that struck at the heart of American freedom. Perhaps that is the way it should be. For if Palmer at times displayed the best that was in the American tradition, in 1920 he very nearly gave it all away in succumbing to the hysteria of the great Red Scare.

Mr. Damon, who for many years has worked as a researcher for AMERICAN HERITAGE, *checking articles for accuracy before publication, teaches history in Chappaqua, New York. He recommends for further reading* A. Mitchell Palmer: Politician, *by Stanley Coben (Columbia University Press, 1963);* Red Scare: a Study in National Hysteria, 1919–1920, *by Robert K. Murray (University of Minnesota Press, 1955); and* The Roots of American Communism, *by Theodore Draper (Viking, 1957).*

Is This Any Way to Ruin a Railroad? CONTINUED FROM PAGE 57

Every idea for attracting passengers back to the railroads or for making it easier to travel by rail was somehow flawed—it was too expensive, too impractical, too likely to be fought by the unions.

In the 1950's one figure glared from every railroad company's balance sheet: the alleged deficits accruing from the passenger service. These deficits were frightful. They were also exceedingly well publicized, for every railroad company had discovered that the sure-pop way to get its weaker trains discontinued was to agitate the public generally and Congress particularly by pleading imminent bankruptcy unless these deficits were wiped out.

In the aggregate, these deficits for the years 1950–57 amounted to over five and one quarter billion dollars. Good grief! How could any industry survive under such a staggering burden? Obviously, none could. The passenger-service deficit, so-called, is and always has been a statistical mirage, a fraud, a phony; most useful, perhaps, as a means of singling out those railroad executives who lie to the public (even, occasionally, to their own shareholders) and betray the public interest with the greatest effrontery.

Over the years their distortions have been designed to convince us all that the carriage of passengers by the railroads is ever and everywhere unprofitable and can be maintained thanks only to the profitable carriage of freight. Their flimflam has been, and still is, based on a venerable formula, prescribed by the Interstate Commerce Commission, by which the railroads are required to separate a set of imprecise costs that are imperfectly understood even by their own officers.

The formula is called "Rules Governing the Separation of Operating Expenses, Railway Taxes, Equipment Rents and Joint Facility Rents Between Freight Service and Passenger Service on Class I Line-Haul Railroads," and as Stanley Berge, professor of transportation at Northwestern University, has pointed out, even the title has a Victorian ring.

The formula was concocted in 1887, when the chief concern was to keep freight rates and passenger fares within reasonable bounds. Cost accounting was both unknown and unnecessary in that time of monopoly, and so the commission required only that the railroads file a schedule separating expenses "chargeable to passenger traffic" from those "chargeable to freight traffic." Expenses chargeable to both services were to be divided in proportion to the train-miles of each service.

Almost at once the formula was assailed by the Association of American Railway Accounting Officers as "an arbitrary rule" that "will furnish misinformation if used . . . for any practical purpose." Soon afterward the formula was savaged by the state railway commissioners as "grossly erroneous, not to say preposterous." Taking the hint, the commission itself retired the formula in 1894, but twenty years later it was revived and elaborated, and it still stands today, more bewildering than ever. In brief, the formula now requires that the railroad companies charge their passenger service with millions of dollars of maintenance and other overhead costs, all of which would still have to be paid if every passenger train vanished tomorrow.

This phantom deficit continued to bother a lot of people, in and out of the industry. A prominent I.C.C. official confessed publicly in 1954 that the commission's estimate was "overstated" by two or three hundred million dollars. Two years later, the governors of the New York Stock Exchange felt sufficiently concerned on behalf of the shareholders to ask for an investigation of the railroads' accounting practices.

The spate of criticism led the I.C.C. to hold hearings in 1957 on the separation rules that had created this bugaboo. More objections were at once voiced, including one from the Post Office Department.

Then something most curious happened. The Association of American Railroads submitted a statement urging, in effect, that the rules be left unchanged. It was a complete turnabout from the association's position two years earlier, when the formula had been derided for producing data "of questionable value." How came this astonishing switch by the association? Easily, quickly, once it had been determined by the lords of the railroads that the phantom deficit was a most useful hobgoblin with which to alarm impressionable congressmen. In 1957 and 1958 they were exerting pressure on Congress to amend the Interstate Commerce Act so that unwanted passenger trains might be more easily lopped off; the bigger the deficit could be made to seem, the sooner Congress would act. The amendment was duly enacted. The butchery of the passenger service proceeded briskly. Between two

and three hundred intercity trains vanished each year.

Now, when a passenger train that moves back and forth between two cities is discontinued, in all likelihood the old-time way of hauling the mail between those two cities has been jeopardized. When several thousand such intercity trains are cancelled, the disruption of mail service is almost complete. Back in 1935 the railroads had operated some ten thousand mail-carrying passenger trains, but by 1959 there were fewer than two thousand passenger trains available to carry the mails, and not all of these were running on schedules that made them useful or attractive to the Post Office Department.

Meanwhile the load of mail had enormously increased and the Post Office was rapidly becoming everybody's favorite whipping boy. With increasing frequency, the Post Office decided to cancel its contracts with the railroads for the handling of bulk mail and to award the contracts instead to truckers and, even for ordinary first-class mail, to the airlines.

Predictably, the railroad executives yelped. On the face of it, their anguish was puzzling: from 1958 through 1964 their mail revenues consistently hovered around $330,000,000 a year; higher than ever before, more than half as much as the revenues for carrying people; more, it would seem, than the railroads deserved to be paid, after so thoroughly discombobulating the mail service. Why then should railroad officials gripe about an occasional cancelled contract?

An answer can be found in one of the earliest plaints, by the Eastern Railroad Presidents Conference, in February, 1958:

At recent hearings in the Interstate Commerce Commission's Passenger Deficit Investigation [said a statement by the conference] it was brought out that frequently the railroads have been forced to discontinue passenger trains because the Post Office Department has taken the mail away.

The unmistakable implication here was that the railroad presidents had been nobly struggling to save the passenger service but that the wicked Post Office had "forced" the defeat of their efforts. This was not true. The commission knew it was not true and said so. The railroad presidents also knew it was not true; one must ruefully conclude that here is another example of their fibbing. Their statement went further:

On top of this, the Post Office Department has been diverting the more profitable mail to airlines and truckers wherever it feels that it will be to its advantage.... The diversion of the more profitable mail traffic away from the railroads will eventually weaken the railroads' ability to provide a national system of mail service and [has] already caused or helped to cause the discontinuance of many passenger trains.

Here was a superb example of a multiple untruth, one that contains in a small compass so much distortion, irrelevance, unwarranted assumption, and flat inaccuracy that it can be properly corrected only by rewriting it entirely and quite changing its meaning and thrust. Yet in the years that have followed, the railroad executives have nurtured this untruth to a luxurious growth, for it perfectly serves their purpose.

At length, the officials at the Post Office came to weary of their role as the bad guys in the steady slaughter of the rail passenger service. They dug back into their files and presently were able to show that, from February 1, 1953, to December 31, 1966, a total of 2,528 mail-carrying passenger trains had been discontinued, of which 1,730 were discontinued after their mail traffic had been removed at the request of the railroads, and 798 were discontinued after their mail traffic had been removed on the initiative of the Post Office.

So all the propaganda from the railroads about the wicked Post Office assays at a little better than thirty per cent accurate—which is, to be sure, a phenomenal batting average for truth in the railroad business.

At all events, it seems clear that the mail revenues provide very inadequate support for a healthy passenger service. On January 1, 1967, only 876 passenger trains carried the mail.

During the early 1960's the industry did little to refurbish or to replace its deteriorating passenger-service equipment, or to make any effort on behalf of its passengers. To be sure, there were still a few companies that welcomed their passengers and afforded them courteous and comfortable service; still a few companies to remind the world that, at their best, American trains are unrivalled; and of these few, one must mention the Seaboard Coast Line for its trains to and from Florida, the Illinois Central for its trains between Chicago and New Orleans, the Great Northern and the Northern Pacific for their limiteds through the northwest, the Burlington and the Union Pacific for their superior limiteds, and the Santa Fe for its fine limiteds through the southwest.

Despite these scattered examples, the millions of Americans who still prefer to travel considerable distances by rail are convinced that the industry has downgraded the passenger service steadily, swiftly, and de-

liberately. They would agree with the analysis of yet another committee that has examined American railroads in detail. In January, 1961, a special study group appointed by the Senate Committee on Interstate and Foreign Commerce concluded, after gloomily inspecting the rail passenger service:

The very age of the railroad coach is one of its worst handicaps. The coach and the people who operate it seem to have forgotten how to change their habits and to have forgotten that innovation and intelligent improvement have been a hallmark of American business since well before the coach's birth.

So matters stood when, in 1962, Senator Pell published his plan, deplored by most railroad executives but hailed with gratitude by despondent rail passengers all over the country. The Pell plan was less important for what it provided than for the discussion it aroused. (The plan envisioned an eight-state public authority, one that was to have owned and operated a high-speed railroad passenger service within Megalopolis—that is, the densely populated region from Boston to Washington; the system was to have been financed by long-term, tax-exempt bonds guaranteed by the government.) No sooner had news of it been published in the *New York Times* than Senator Pell sensed that he had struck a vein of purest political gold. Congratulatory letters poured into his office, and his proposal received extraordinarily friendly editorial comment in newspapers all over the country. Pell was encouraged; he was also persistent, and kept pressing the White House for executive action. He nagged, he pestered, and he could marshal battalions of disconcerting facts.

At first nothing much happened, for the Highway Users Conference (which boasts a lobby second only to the Pentagon's in its influence on Capitol Hill) and the airlines were both suspicious, and the railroad industry was conspicuously indifferent. In the last year of the Kennedy administration, $1,000,000 was asked and $625,000 was actually authorized to study the assumptions underlying the Pell plan, now officially known as the Northeast Corridor Project; in the first year of the Johnson administration, after much prodding by Pell, the Secretary of Commerce announced an ambitious research and development program for high-speed passenger transportation.

In January, 1965, in his report to Congress on the state of the Union, President Johnson said, "I will ask for funds to study high-speed rail transportation between urban centers. We will begin with test projects between Boston and Washington. On high-speed trains, passengers could travel this distance in less than four hours." *Four hours?* Those unhappy people who still travelled by rail between Boston and Wash-

ington were used to the fact that if all went well—which it seldom did—the trip took eight hours and forty minutes. Yet the President reckoned it should take less than four hours? When *that* came to pass, his would not be merely a Great Society, it would be a Naked Miracle.

The administration's bill, which authorized ninety million dollars for new passenger equipment and further research, slid easily through Congress, assisted now by the Railway Progress Institute (the association of railway equipment manufacturers, each of whom was eager for a contract), by the steel industry, by the railway labor unions, and, *mirabile dictu,* by the railroads. Stuart Saunders of the Pennsylvania urged passage of the bill and said he knew of no railroad official who implacably opposed it. After all, the only railroads directly involved in the Northeast Corridor Project were the Pennsylvania and the bankrupt New Haven.

On September 30, 1965, before a throng of congressmen, railroad presidents, and other dignitaries assembled in the East Room of the White House, President Johnson ceremoniously signed the High-Speed Ground Transportation Act. A big moment; a speech. Ritual pens handed out, hands shaken, smiles exchanged, a buzz of happy talk. The congressmen took their leave, among them Senator Pell, who had glittered briefly in the presidential spotlight; but the railroad presidents lingered, awaiting their cue.

At the President's chummy invitation, the railroad men then moved to another room of the White House, where he talked with them for a time in the persuasive manner for which he is celebrated. The performance was private, but some of those who were present later sketched, with some awe, its main features. The President praised them warmly for bringing their companies through a time of lean pickings, expressed concern over the problems posed by their competition, wagged his head over the difficulties of regulation, mentioned the profits flooding in on the wave of current prosperity, and commented that the railroads

were unexcelled at carrying large numbers of people from here to there. Then, in a marked manner, came the presidential request: any further reductions in the passenger service must at all costs be avoided. Did they not agree that it was essential to keep the passenger service at its current level? Perhaps even to restore some of the trains that had already been discontinued?

At this point, some of his guests seemed rather uncomfortable. The President suggested that he would like to see a report on the whole question of the passenger service, its future, how it could be made to work—and who better to prepare such a report than the leaders of the industry?

Before they left, the railroad men had agreed to reconsider the problem of the passenger service and report back in three months—by January, 1966.

However inopportune, here was another of those magic occasions when the railroad men had the chance to obliterate the errors and stupidities of the past; no questions asked, no blames assessed, no guilts imputed. If they had treated their passengers shabbily, the public, through its elected representatives, had agreed to forget all the old animosities and had whipped up a good deal of excitement over the brave new trains promised for the future. If the government in Washington had treated the railroads unfairly, if federal funds had been inequitably sluiced to their competitors, now the seasons had wheeled through an equinox, and at last the railroads were once again sharing in these federal bounties.

Moreover, if they chose so to construe the President's request, the railroad men had just to the north of them a spectacular example of how they might revive the passenger service, modernize it, and make it both popular and profitable: the example of the Canadian National.

The C.N. is the world's biggest railroad, operating more than 32,000 miles of track through all ten Canadian provinces and into some of the northern United States as well. Unlike its chief competitor, the Canadian Pacific, the C.N. has been nationalized since 1919, but it is still highly competitive. During the 1950's, in the best tradition of orthodox railroad management, the C.N. discontinued one quarter of its passenger service, and would have dropped more had not the Canadian Board of Transport Commissioners in 1961 blown the whistle on such practices.

The effect of this caveat on the C.N. was remarkable. If it was stuck with a passenger business, by Heaven, it would try to make it pay. Fares were slashed—first experimentally and then all over the dominion—as much as fifty per cent. Modern trains began to move on faster schedules; tickets were offered by mail and on credit; a Car-Go-Rail plan enabled

passengers to take their automobiles and find them, freshly washed, at their destination. The public flocked aboard the C.N. trains, especially the Rapido, which runs from Montreal to Toronto.

The Rapido went into service in October, 1965, and at once became the fastest intercity train in North America, running the 335 miles in five hours, which was eighty-five minutes faster than the train it had replaced. A first-class ticket, which included an excellent dinner, was fifteen dollars; a coach seat cost eight dollars; the combination of comfort, service, and dependability proved so popular that it soon became necessary to reserve space a week in advance. (By contrast, the New York Central's Chicagoan takes six hours to run the same distance from Cleveland to Chicago; first-class costs $25.74; coach is $16.25; all meals are extra; and there is no rush to clamber aboard the train.)

The C.N. has now announced that the Rapido will in turn be replaced by five turbine-powered trains, built of aluminum and specially designed to ride smoothly at speeds up to one hundred and sixty miles an hour, further reducing the time of the Toronto–Montreal run to *four* hours. Moreover, the railroad is confident that these turbo-trains will make the C.N.'s passenger service profitable by 1970.

Was there here a lesson for American railroad executives? Or could they learn anything from the resounding success of the Japanese Tokaido line, which shoots a handsome train called the Bullet 320 miles between Tokyo and Osaka in *three* hours? Possibly; but the chief executive officers of the great American railroad companies have on their minds more exigent matters than the performance of passenger trains in foreign countries. They delegated the task of drafting the report for President Johnson to their general counsels and the Association of American Railroads.

In due course the report ("On the Intercity Rail Passenger Train Situation, and Certain Other Railroad Problems") was approved, neatly typed, and, on January 5, 1966, delivered to the White House. It was a pedestrian document; a rambling recapitulation of all the industry's fancied grievances against regulators, tax assessors, tax legislators, competitors, and the architects of the so-called federal transportation policy; and yet, as the months passed and their report provoked no official reaction, the railroad men bridled. They believed they had proffered substantial pledges and had also suggested, discreetly, that their posture on fundamental issues was radically altered. Why then were their tenders ignored?

In the face of a frosty silence at the White House, the railroad men themselves made public their revolutionary about-face. It was that they no longer insisted on the absurd estimate of the mythical passenger deficit computed by the commission's formula (which in 1965 amounted to $421,000,000); they now admitted that their actual out-of-pocket losses amounted to only $44,000,000. (Even this estimate is probably exaggerated.) The broad implication was that any administration which wished to preserve the passenger service in its status quo, and which at the same time was paying out zillions of dollars of federal funds to

build highways and to subsidize airlines, could easily afford to pick up the tab for such a trivial deficit.

But the White House declined to jump at the bait. Obviously the report was not the "imaginative solution" to the rail passenger service problem that President Johnson had sought.

Stalemate.

On October 3, 1966, one year after the High-Speed Ground Transportation Act had been signed, Senator Pell was pleased to invite the attention of his colleagues to a report of what had been done to improve the rail passenger service in the Northeast Corridor. Some brave first steps had been taken.

A program of research and development had been launched, with emphasis on railroad technology but geared to explore some fairly unconventional high-speed systems as well. Experimental cars were to be built, crammed with hundreds of electronic sensors and other delicate instrumentation, and set to testing every imaginable aspect of high-speed rail transportation, from the depth of ballast in the roadbed to the

interaction of pantograph and catenary in the overhead grid of electric cables; this time nothing was to be left to chance or guesswork.

The lessons of all this belated research were to be embodied in three demonstration projects. One is designed to explore the feasibility of hauling passengers *and* their automobiles, in specially designed double-decked railroad cars, from Alexandria to Jacksonville over the tracks of the Seaboard Coast Line. Once on board the train, passengers will be able to get out of their automobiles, stroll about, leave their children to romp in supervised play areas, relax in a lounge car, watch television, and eat in a cafeteria car. The trip will take about twelve hours. The demonstration is to begin sometime this year.

The other two demonstration projects were, of course, designed to speed and otherwise improve rail travel in the Northeast Corridor; and in these Senator Pell could take an almost paternal pride. Both projects are scheduled to be in experimental operation early this year.

Because of the deplorable financial condition of the New Haven, the demonstration project between Boston and New York is necessarily limited in scope. Moreover, the tracks of the New Haven curve and wind along the shore line, meandering over 129 grade crossings and 179 bridges which are from fifty to seventy-five years old. The road itself is in wretched condition. How could anyone imagine that trains could be moved over it fast enough to clip an hour from the time the trip has always taken? The challenge was accepted by the United Aircraft Corporation Systems Center. The company has designed and built two small, very light train sets of three cars each, powered by aircraft turbine engines that weigh only 250 pounds apiece, and has suspended the trains so that they swing inward as they bank around curves. Thus they are able to negotiate curves thirty per cent faster than trains of conventional design. (Here is another instance of the engineering ingenuity so conspicuously lacking in the railroad industry for so many decades.) The United Aircraft train sets can zip along at 150 m.p.h. over the New Haven's existing tracks, but they will be held to about 110 m.p.h. The state of Connecticut, through its Transportation Authority, has paid out $500,000 to make structural improvements in the roadbed. The federal government, through the new Department of Transportation, has made contracts with the New Haven, specifying standards of on-time performance, cleanliness, and those other considerations necessary for a proper test of public reaction to the experimental service.

It is, however, the demonstration project between New York and Washington, over the tracks of the

Pennsylvania, that affords the richest promise for a better rail passenger service not only in the Northeast Corridor but all over the country. This is because the officers of the Pennsylvania are sharply aware that everybody in the railroad business, indeed everybody in the transportation business, in this country and abroad, is taking a lively interest in just what kind of a passenger service the Pennsylvania will offer after so many years of slovenliness and neglect. And anyone who thinks that in these circumstances the Pennsylvania Railroad Company will not try its damnedest to do its best simply does not know the Pennsylvania Railroad Company.

The outward and visible signs of this inward and corporate grace are an improved catenary system, two hundred thousand tons of ballast for a stronger roadbed, hundreds of miles of continuous welded rail, four reinforced bridges, and raised platforms in the depots at Washington, Baltimore, and Wilmington— a list of items that cost the Pennsylvania more than twenty-five million dollars. Other visible signs are the fifty cars—ten parlor cars and forty coaches, twenty of them equipped with quick-service food counters— carpeted, quiet, and comfortable. They are self-propelled, able to cruise at 150 m.p.h., coupled in pairs, operating in trains of four, six, eight, or more, and capable of slicing about an hour off the old time. They cost the railroad more than eleven million dollars.

The demonstration is to run for two years, during which the railroad has agreed (by contract with the Department of Transportation) to experiment with the price of fares, the schedule of stops at intermediate depots, the kind of meals to be served, methods of selling tickets and making reservations, and the possibilities offered by on-board entertainments of various kinds. Those railroad employees who deal with passengers will have been schooled in such old-fashioned virtues as courtesy. Thirty of the cars have telephones; the system permits passengers to receive calls as well as make them. The trains may run on even swifter schedules during the last phase of the demonstration, perhaps fast enough to speed between Washington and New York in two hours and twenty minutes, every hour on the hour.

The aggressive co-operation of the Pennsylvania with the Office of High-Speed Ground Transportation does not mean that Stuart Saunders, the Pennsylvania's chief executive officer, has suddenly moved to the Amen corner and will now whoop it up for the passenger service; he is still inimical to the long-distance passenger train, and he regards the commuter train with considerable loathing; but he deplores our irrational, wasteful devotion to the automobile. ("We are blacktopping ourselves to death," he has said. "The

cloverleaf has become our national flower.") Thus he perceived an economic justification for expanding rail passenger service in a densely populated, 226-mile strip of urban sprawl.

The pressure on other carriers is already mounting. In January, 1967, a group of civic and state organizations held a Midwest High-Speed Rail Transit Conference in Chicago; a paper was read by Robert A. Nelson, the able and imaginative director of the Northeast Corridor Project; another paper, by W. W. Hay, professor of railway civil engineering at the University of Illinois, argued that in the relatively flat Midwest, after a few technical improvements, the time of trips between St. Louis and Chicago could be reduced from five and one half to three hours; the Twin Cities and Chicago, from six and one half to four and one half hours; Detroit and Chicago, from five and

one half to three hours; and Cleveland and Chicago, from six to three and one half hours. "These improved times," Hay said, "would all be competitive with modern jet air schedules."

It is worth noting that the railroads have long been technologically capable of operating trains at high speeds. Thirty years ago trains of the Chicago & North Western, the Burlington, and the Milwaukee Road all regularly hit 100 m.p.h. on the run between Chicago and the Twin Cities; fifty years ago speeds of more than 100 m.p.h. were routine for passenger trains on straight, level stretches of track; in 1905 a train of the Pennsylvania Railroad attained 127 m.p.h. over three miles of track in western Ohio. Trains are slower today only because the companies that operate them have deliberately downgraded the service.

Not that the debate about public transportation will ever be resolved to everyone's satisfaction.

In terms of efficiency, of safety and dependability in all weathers, and of financial economy, the railroads are first and their competitors nowhere in sight; but in an affluent, spendthrift society, such arguments as efficiency and economy carry little weight.

What counts in this debate are incontrovertible facts like the steady deterioration of the fleet of passenger cars and the appalling cost of replacing that fleet. If a determination of public policy is not made very soon, there will be no more rail passenger service simply because the cars to carry passengers will be too decrepit for the demands made upon them. To tempt the large sums of capital (public as well as private) needed to build and buy a fleet of new, comfortable, clean, quiet passenger cars, there must be unmistakable evidence of a public demand for an improved rail passenger service, and the demonstration project in the Northeast Corridor, it is hoped, will supply such evidence in abundance.

It may be doubted that the railroad companies will undertake any such service unless the federal government makes it quite clear that they will be allowed to cancel no more intercity trains, that they are in the passenger business to stay. But even if the industry succeeds in uneducating the public, even if new equipment is put into service, tracks and roadbeds are improved, and schedules speeded up, everything in our past experience shows that the passenger service nationally will have to be supervised or at least sharply scrutinized by an appropriate federal agency, just as the conduct of the demonstration projects in the Northeast Corridor is now being supervised by the Office of High-Speed Ground Transportation.

Surveillance is mandatory, for the business of railroading is in truth two quite different businesses—the hauling of freight and the carriage of people—with quite different managerial functions. The hauling of freight is a wholesale, industrial function. It has been well described as a factory that produces transportation in trainload lots for a relatively few customers, the shippers; this factory also functions for the same few customers as a mobile warehouse. The carriage of people, however, is a retail function, more like a specialty shop that sells custom-made goods to an exacting clientele. To ask one man to manage both enterprises is rather like asking the same actor to perform roles written for, say, John Wayne and Doris Day. Moreover, since the revenues from the passenger service in 1961–65 were only about thirteen per cent of the revenues from the freight service, it is not hard to guess how the one manager of both services will

spend his time and his energy and his capital funds—unless an unwinking eye is on him, watchful lest he give less than his wholehearted and zestful best on behalf of his passenger service.

And if the masters of the railroads resist such supervision, if they complain of further intolerable regulation, they must be reminded of what they have studiously ignored and hoped everybody else has forgotten, that the railways are public highways, laid down for the convenience of the general public, required to respond equably and equitably to the public necessity, and administered—at least theoretically—in the public interest. Eighty years ago, in the full wrath of our sovereign majesty, we decreed that the railroads must be regulated by a public authority, the Interstate Commerce Commission, and ever since, the masters of the railroads have attempted to squirm out from under this authority, to subvert it, or to overthrow it. Now that we have built other highways on the ground and invented still others to fill the air, we have grown careless of our dominion and permitted, without rebuff, an insolence from those who administer the railed public highways. In this way, through their contumacy on the one hand and a reckless squandering of our sovereign power on the other, we have reached a crisis in the business and the pleasure of travelling from here to there and back again.

In this crisis, time is a factor that can no longer be controlled. The equipment to operate a national passenger service has been allowed to deteriorate beyond patchwork: it is no longer obsolescent or even obsolete; it is all but extinct. No longer do we have a choice. We must once again exert our sovereign power. We must bid our government rule that the railed highways shall remain open for passengers. Once the masters of the railroads have been given orders in unmistakable terms, they must find ways to revive the passenger service. If they cannot, they must be relieved of the responsibility, and the passenger service must be nationalized.

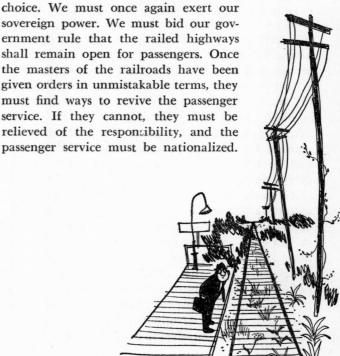

Peter Lyon, a New York-based free-lance writer, is a veteran contributor to AMERICAN HERITAGE. *His first book,* Success Story: The Life and Times of S. S. McClure, *is a biography of his late grandfather. The cartoons accompanying this article are by James Stevenson of* The New Yorker.

Mission to Spain

CONTINUED FROM PAGE 11

the Continental Congress in the West Indies] was still at St. Pierre; when we arrived opposite to that City Mr. Jay wrote him a letter, and my brother waited upon him; upon which Mr. Bingham very politely returned with the Colonel and insisted upon our resideing with him during our stay at Martinique; and never was I more charmed with any thing of the kind than with the polite friendly reception we met with from that gentleman. The two families most dear to me would be delighted with this Island. The neatness that prevails here cannot be exceeded and frankly I confess I never saw it equalled.

How mistaken was I as to the character of our allies! The Admiral Le Motte Piquet has granted to Mr. Gerard's request a Frigate to convey us to France, and we shall sail from this place the 28th inst. . . .

And now I must bid adieu to my best beloved friends. Think not any more that I have forgotten you. . . .

May the Almighty guard, protect and bless, my ever dear, my ever valued friends. Embrace my little blessing [young Peter Augustus]. My heart is too sensibly affected to proceed, and to discontinue is like parting a new. Adieu!

SA. JAY

A brief description of Martinique and of the second leg of the journey, from Martinique to Spain, is furnished by Jay in a letter to Robert R. Livingston written shortly after his arrival in Cadiz. Now that he was actually in Spain, he thought it prudent to adopt a slightly more complicated code for his correspondence with his friend.

Cadiz, 19th February 1780

Dear Robert

. . . We left Martinico the 28th December in the Aurora a French Frigate commanded by [Admiral La Motte-Picquet] a very genteel agreeable Man. He went by the Way of St. Thomas to avoid Danger [from the British fleet]; and arrived here the 22d of last Month. If when you have nothing else to do, you should consult your Map, you will percieve that we had a very uncommon short Passage. The Aurora is a dull Sailor, but we were favored with Winds constantly fair, and I may add strong. The Marquis was bound to Toulon, from whence we expected to have gone to Paris, and from thence over the Pyrenees to Madrid. But on touching here for Intelligence, we learned that Admiral [Sir George] Rodney had saved us the neces-

sity of going that round about Way to Madrid, he having gained an undoubted Superiority in the Mediterranean. This Point being settled, I immediately made the necessary Communications to the Spanish Ministry, from whom I am now in daily Expectation of recieving Dispatches.

The Cypher I sent you has become useless, and must be omitted. Take the following, vizt. the second part of Boyers Dictionary, in which the English is placed before the French. It is not paged. You will therefore number the Pages, marking the first page with No. 1, and so on. In each page there are three Columns— let *c* denote the first, *a* the second, and *b* third. Count the number of words from the Top, to the one you mean to use, inclusive, and add seven to it. Thus, for Instance, the word *abject* is the *third* word, in the *third* Column, of the *second* Page; and is to be written in Cypher as follows—2-b-10. The Dictionary I have was printed in London in the Year 1771 and is called the thirteenth Edition with large additions.

. . . Be particular in informing me whether this Letter comes to your Hands free from Marks of Inspection. I shall put a Wafer under the Seal; compare the Impression with those you have formerly recieved from me. If you should have Reason to suspect that all is not fair, I will on being informed of it send you another Cypher. Be cautious what you write in the common Way, as I am persuaded few Letters would reach me thro the Post Offices of France or Spain uninspected.

Be so kind as to present our Regards and best Wishes to your Mama, Mrs. Livingston and the Rest of the Family.

I am Dear Robert
Your Friend
JOHN JAY

Since Jay was uncertain whether or not the court at Madrid was prepared to give him accreditation as a minister plenipotentiary from the thirteen rebellious American states, he prudently stayed at Cadiz and dispatched the secretary of the mission, William Carmichael, to proceed to the capital and report back. Unlike Jay, Carmichael had a passable command of Spanish. He was also a clever and ambitious intriguer —Jay did not, in fact, entirely trust him—with some background in the handling of Congress's business in Europe. In the long run, however, he was to prove a good deal more affable and resilient in dealing with the Spaniards than his unbending and righteous superior; when Jay was called to Paris at the end of his mission in Spain, Carmichael succeeded him as American representative at Madrid.

Unfortunately for Jay, he followed Gérard's advice

and instructed Carmichael to make his overtures to *Don José de Gálvez* (spelled "Galvaise" by Jay), Minister of the Indies, the Spanish equivalent of Colonial Secretary; in fact, the Conde de Floridablanca, the excitable foreign minister and principal adviser of Charles III, regarded the American negotiations as his private preserve. Thus, ineptly, the mission got off on the wrong foot. It was not helped by an over-optimistic scouting report from Carmichael, who told Jay that all was well between Spain and America's ally, France, and implied that Jay himself would be well received at court. Thus encouraged, Jay set out with his family in a mule-drawn carriage on the dusty, four-hundred-mile journey from Cadiz to Madrid, passing through country immortalized in **Don Quixote de la Mancha,** suffering the discomforts of Spanish inns, and observing the rural life captured by Goya in his immortal canvases of the Spanish countryside (see pages 12 through 15).

They reached the handsomely laid out capital on April 4, 1780. Jay quickly learned that neither the frugal and pious Charles III nor the Conde de Floridablanca had any intention of recognizing the independence of the United States until England was defeated. Not only that, but the Spanish king and his foreign minister even had regrets about France's precipitate action in making an alliance with America, and had begun to reappraise the military value of their own alliance with their Bourbon partner. The Spanish government, with its own vast colonial empire in the New World, did not approve of revolutions, certainly not of successful ones. Instead of independence, Floridablanca preferred to see the American revolutionaries forced to accept the status of feudal dependencies of George III, a status comparable to the relation between the central European states and the Empire of Maria Theresa.

Jay set up an establishment in San Mateo Street, but was soon to be engaged in following the court from country seat to country seat, for Charles III, to pursue the pleasures of the hunt, would move from his winter capital of El Pardo, just nine miles from Madrid, to Aranjuez, some twenty-six miles from Madrid, and then to the north at the two sites of El Escorial and San Ildefonso. Sally Jay, who was then pregnant, stayed in Madrid. Her husband, cooped up in Aranjuez in a single room in a dingy boarding house, gives us a shocking picture of the straits to which America's unaccredited minister plenipotentiary was reduced. He confided his feelings to Livingston.

Madrid 23 May 1780

Dear Robert.

...I am here in a disagreable Situation. Congress

On the French island of Martinique, where they refitted after a storm at sea, the Jays were shocked by the slave trade. In later years Mr. Jay was an outspoken abolitionist.

have made me no Remittances—the small Credit I had on Doctr. [Benjamin] Franklin [then in Paris] is expended. The Idea of being maintained by the Court of Spain is humiliating, and therefore not for the public Good. The Salary allowed me is greatly inadequate—no part of Europe is so expensive—nor did I ever live so oeconomically. The Court is never stationary—moving from Madrid to the Pardo, then to Aranjues—thence to St. El Defonso—thence to the Escurial—in perpetual Rotation. To keep a House at each place is not within the Limits of my Finances—to take ready furnished Lodgings and keep my own Table at each, is beyond Belief expensive. I live at Aranjues, in a Posada [inn], in one single Room, with but one Servant, and without a Carriage. When I left Philadelphia every thing was cheaper there than here. Spain does not cloath its Inhabitants—their Butter Cheese fine Linnen, fine Silks, and fine Cloths, come from France Holland etc. They have imposed an exorbitant Duty on all foreign Commodities, and a heavy Tax is laid on Eatables sold in the Market. The Sum allowed me will let me live, but not as I ought to do—a paltry post Chaise drawn by three Mules costs me every Time I go to or from here to Aranjues (7 Leagues) ten Dollars—all things in that Proportion. To Day I am to try a pair of Mules for which I am asked 480 Dollars—they tell me they are very cheap. Yesterday I refused a pair, the Price of which was 640 Dollars. I cannot get a plain decent Carriage and

Harness under 870 Dollars. Judge of my Situation—so circumstanced I cannot employ Couriers to carry my Dispatches to the Sea Side or to France. My Letters by the Post are all opened. Fortunately on this occasion Mr. [Richard] Harrison [American agent at Cadiz, whom Jay often used as an unofficial courier] now going to Cadiz will take my Letters. With whatever Allowance Congress may make, I shall be content. I know how and am determined to live agreable to my Circumstances. If Inconveniences result from their being too narrow, they will be public ones. They therefore merit the Consideration of Congress....

I am your Friend
John Jay*

Jay did not come face to face with Floridablanca until May 11, 1780, almost four months after arriving at Cadiz, but a considerable correspondence preceded the confrontation. From the Pardo, Floridablanca had informed Jay at the end of February that until the bases for an alliance with Spain were disclosed, his Majesty felt that it would not be "proper" for Jay "to assume a formal character, which must depend on a public acknowledgment and future treaty." "Divested of the gloss which its politeness spreads over it," Jay informed the president of Congress, Floridablanca's pronouncement meant that the United States would be recognized only when and if it agreed to certain terms. Gérard had warned Jay that Congress's insistence on America's sharing the navigation of the Mississippi might well prove a stumbling block, but Jay was not willing to drop this demand. "As affairs are now circumstanced," he wrote Congress, "it would, in my opinion, be better for America to have no treaty with Spain than to purchase one on such servile terms. There was a time when it might have been proper to have given that country something for their making common cause with us, but that day is now past. Spain is at war with Britain."

Floridablanca, preliminary to a meeting, asked Jay for a lengthy report on "the civil and military state of the American provinces"—he could not bring himself to say "states"—and their resources. Jay labored over his reply for several weeks until he had amassed and organized an impressive body of data.

Then, late in April, Jay learned that some months before, Congress, jumping the gun in anticipation of a loan from Spain, had drawn bills of exchange upon Jay for 100,000 pounds sterling payable at sight in six months; only a month now remained before the bills would fall due, and Jay was reduced to the humilia-

* This letter is published by permission of the New-York Historical Society.

tion of informing Floridablanca of their existence and asking for immediate payment. In his letter Jay conceded that Congress's action might appear "indelicate," but offered as an excuse the impossibility of notifying the King earlier because of his own protracted voyage to Spain.

Accordingly, it was a wary foreign minister who confronted John Jay in person at Aranjuez, where the court was staying, on May 11, 1780. The Conde de Floridablanca was, like his American visitor, a man of middle-class background bred to the law. Fifteen years Jay's senior, he was as vain as the New Yorker and had already won a reputation both for ruthlessness to political rivals and for a temper that could not brook contradiction.

Jay spoke no Spanish, Floridablanca no English. In this and future conferences between the two, Carmichael acted as translator; immediately afterward he would sit down and commit what had been said to paper. In this way Jay kept a running account of his meetings with the Foreign Minister, which he sent to Congress along with comments of his own. Those that have hitherto appeared in print have been inaccurately reproduced, and significant cipher portions, herein decoded, have in the past been omitted.

As the two diplomats spoke, Jay soon realized that the Spaniards expected a quid *for the* quo *he sought.*

Aranjuez 11th May 1780

... [Floridablanca] observed that he intended to speak on two Points. The first related to the Letter Mr. Jay had written to him, on the Subject of Bills of Exchange drawn on him by Congress.... He said that the last Year he should have found no Difficulty on that Head, but that at present, although Spain had Money, she was in the Situation of Tantalus, who with Water in View could not make use of it—alluding to the Revenue arising from their Possessions in America, which they were not able to draw from thence [because of the British blockade]. That their Expenses in the year 1779 had been so great, particularly for the Marine, as to oblige them to make large Loans, which they were negotiating at present. He entered into a Summary of those Expenses, and particularized the enormous Expense of supporting thirty five Ships of the Line and Frigates in French Ports.

Floridablanca was referring to an ill-fated Franco-Spanish naval armada assembled in the summer of 1779 to spearhead an invasion of England. Plagued by a smallpox epidemic and by mismanagement for which both allies shared the blame, the joint fleet maneuvered ineffectively in the Channel waters until good sailing weather was gone, and the invasion fizzled out.

This joined to the other Expenses . . . rendered it difficult for the King to do for America what he could have done easily in the last Year. . . . yet that it was his Majesty's Intentions to give America all the Assistance in his Power. . . .

In order to facilitate this, he said it was necessary to make some overtures for a Contract . . . and then he pointed out the object most essential to the Interests of Spain at the present Conjuncture. He said that for their Marine they wanted light Frigates, Cutters, or swift sailing Vessels of that Size. . . . He also mentioned Timber for Vessels, but said that was an Article, which was not so immediately necessary, though it might be an Object of Consequence in future. . . .

With respect to the Bills of Exchange which might be presented, he said that at the End of the present Year or in the Beginning of the next, he would have it in his Power to advance 25,000, 30,000 or 40,000 Pounds Sterling, and in the mean Time, should these Bills be presented for Payment, he would take such measures as would satisfy the owners of them Vizt., By engaging in the Name of his Majesty to pay them, observing that the Kings good Faith and Credit, was so well known, that he did not imagine this would be a difficult matter. . . .

The Count then proceeded to the second Point Vizt., with Respect to the Treaty in Contemplation between Spain and America. . . . He . . . [observed] That there was but one obstacle, from which he apprehended any great Difficulty in forming a Treaty with America, and plainly intimated that this arose from the Pretensions of America to the Navigation of the Mississippi. He repeated the Information which the Court had received from Monsieur Miralles [Juan de Miralles, Spanish agent to the Continental Congress at Philadelphia], that Congress had at one Time relinquished that Object; That he also knew from the same Source that afterwards they had made it an essential Point of the Treaty. He expressed his uneasiness on this Subject, and entered largely into the Views of Spain with respect to the Boundaries (He . . . expressed their Resolution if possible of excluding the English entirely from the Gulf of Mexico.) they wished to fix by a Treaty which he hoped would be perpetual between the two Countries. He spoke amply of the King's anxiety, Resolution and Firmness on this Point, and insinuated a wish that some method might be fallen upon to remove this Obstacle. . . .

Mr. Jay here took an Opportunity to mention that many of the States were bounded by that River, and were highly interested in its Navigation, but observed that they were equally inclined to enter into any amicable Regulations, which might prevent any Inconveniences with Respect to Contraband or other Objects which might excite the Uneasiness of Spain.

The Count still however appeared to be fully of Opinion that this was an Object that the King had so much at Heart, that he would never relinquish it; adding however that he hoped some middle Way might be hit on which would pave the way to get over this Difficulty and desired Mr. Jay to turn his thoughts and attention to the Subject. . . .

From that initial conference at Aranjuez on May 11, it was apparent to Jay that he was in for a series of fencing matches with a master of thrust, parry, and deception. It was also clear to him that Spain had financial troubles of her own, and furthermore that Congress's insistence on obtaining for America the free navigation of the Mississippi would prove the major stumbling block to a treaty.

Meanwhile, Jay was becoming suspicious of the presence at the Spanish court of Father Thomas Hussey, an Irish priest, and of an English playwright named Richard Cumberland. Cumberland was particularly conspicuous; with his wife and two flirtatious daughters he had taken a large house in Madrid and was openly received at court and presented with gifts by the King. For a nation at war with England to be so ostentatiously cordial to an Englishman, Jay reflected, was very odd indeed; the contrast with his own poor-relation status was painful. Evidently Jay's suspicions reached Floridablanca, possibly through the French ambassador, the Comte de Montmorin. The result was that the Foreign Minister asked Jay and Carmichael to confer with him in his office on the evening of June 2.

Aranjues, 2d June 1780
. . . [Floridablanca said] that his reason for desiring to see [Jay] at present, proceeded from something mentioned to him by the French Ambassador, of which he supposed he was Informed. He recapitulated what he had before mentioned of the Kings good Faith, and favorable disposition towards America. . . . After these reflections and assurances, He told Mr. Jay that the Person lately from England by the way of Portugal [Father Hussey] was the Chaplain of their Former Embassy at London, that he had been there for some time on his private Affairs, and had at the same Time Instructions concerning an exchange of Prisoners, which their sufferings rendered expedient, that the Death of an Uncle, a Chaplain of the Court had obliged him to return. That an English Gentleman and his Family [Cumberland] had come to Lisbon with him under the pretext or really on Account of the Ill Health of a Daughter, to whom the Duke of Dorset was much attached; That the opposition

made by his friends to the marriage had affected her Health, and that this Family was desirous of passing through Spain to Italy. He added that this Gentleman was one of Lord George Germaine's [the British Colonial Secretary] Secretaries, and would perhaps have some proposals to make for an exchange of Prisoners, and possibly others of a different Nature, which he assured Mr. Jay should be communicated to him ... candidly.... He desired Mr. Jay, therefore to make himself easy on this Subject giving new assurances of the King's strict regard to Justice and good Faith and of his disposition to assist America.

Mr. Jay begged him to be persuaded of the perfect confidence of America, and his own, and of their reliance on the good Faith, Justice, and Honor of his Catholic Majesty; that he had no other apprehension from the circumstance of English mens resorting to

Charles himself completed the royal palace at Madrid—it is now the Palacio Nacional—taking possession in 1764.

this Court, than that the enemy would on this, as on former occasions avail themselves of it, by endeavoring to alarm and deceive our People....

Floridablanca was disingenuous in his remarks to Jay about Hussey and Cumberland. The facts seem to show that the intriguing Irish priest was a double agent working for both Spain and England. He and the time-serving English playwright had been authorized by the British Foreign Office to enter into secret talks with Spain to win that nation away from her alliance with France and thus scotch any chance of Spain's recognition of the rebellious Thirteen Colonies. The Cumberland-Hussey negotiations finally bogged down over the issue of Gibraltar, which England had seized in 1704. Spain demanded its return; England refused to allow Cumberland to offer it. Jay, however, was unable to capitalize on that eventuality.

In the ensuing days, Floridablanca seemed evasive.

Jay, now reconciled to protracted negotiations, reported to John Adams: "This Court seems to have great respect for the old adage festina lente, *at least as applied to our independence." Much as he would like to see "perfect amity and cordial affection" between America and her Spanish neighbors, he could not take such an eventuality for granted. "I shall in all my letters advise Congress to rely principally on themselves; to fight out their own cause at any hazard, with spirit, and not to rely too much on the expectation of events which may never happen."*

A few days later Floridablanca alluded once more to the proposal, made in the opening conference, that America supply warships in return for Spanish funds. Jay promptly rejoined that timber, masts, and naval stores as well as labor cost money, the last being one commodity in short supply with Congress. Should the United States put the money advanced by Spain into building frigates for her, the net gain to America would be nil. Should, in the meantime, Congress's bills be protested, would it not deal a blow to the credit of the United States? Would it not be calculated to allow the enemy to draw conclusions as to "the inability of Spain to advance the sum in question?" In a follow-up note to Floridablanca, Jay was completely frank. "Believe me, sir," he wrote, "the United States will not be able to pay their debts during the war, and therefore any plan whatever calculated on a contrary position must be fruitless." He was prepared to pledge the faith of the United States for repayment with "a reasonable interest," after the war, of such sums as might be loaned by Spain. "What more can I offer? What more can they do?" he pleaded. Once more Floridablanca made it clear that there was one thing the United States could do: renounce its claims to the navigation of the Mississippi.

In a niggardly gesture Floridablanca informed Jay that the King was prepared to pay a bill of $333 which Jay had presented, but, as Jay observed to Congress, the Minister's note "looked dry, and indicated a degree of irritation." Jay felt that this was no time to press for the treaty, and he found himself reduced to the role of a humble supplicant for funds to pay bills Congress had recklessly drawn against him for supplies from abroad. A conference with Floridablanca on July 5 followed hard on the heels of the news reaching Madrid that Charleston had fallen to the British. "The effect of it," Jay remarked in a letter to the president of Congress, "was as visible the next day as that of a hard night's frost on young leaves."

Madrid, July the 5th, 1780
...After the usual compliments the bad News relative to the surrender of Charlestown, just received,

became the Topic of conversation. The Count ... expressed his Sorrow on the occasion, but ... seemed to think it strange that the place had not been better defended, and that more vigorous measures had not been taken to impede the Enemy's progress ... Mr. Jay replied that probably when all circumstances relative to this Affair were known, there might be reasons which would account for the conduct of the Americans on this occasion; to the Truth of which remark the Count appeared to assent. [Floridablanca] mentioned the death of Mr. Miralles [at Washington's Morristown encampment at the end of April] and regretted his loss at this time.... He said he had recommended to his Majesty a Person to succeed him, whom he knew, that spoke English whom he expected soon, and to whom he would explain his Ideas on the Subject of the Bills, and on other matters, touching which

Charles III summered at the Escorial, a combined school, monastery, mausoleum, and royal residence built by Philip II. In its Panteón de los Reyes eleven kings, including Charles and the last one, Alfonso XIII (d. 1940), lie buried.

Mr. Jay had written to him, and who would confer also with Mr. Jay on those Subjects....

He then proceeded to speak of the Bills of exchange, in the possession of the Messrs. Joyce [a mercantile house of Bilbao], and seemed to be surprised that that House should be possessed of so many of them. He advised Mr. Jay to be cautious of those Gentlemen, saying that they were as much English in their Hearts, as the Ministry of that Country; ... [Floridablanca then] spoke much of the deranged State of our Finances, and Credit, of the advantages taken of Congress by Merchants and others, who availed themselves of that circumstance, which he called cruel Extortions....

He asked Mr. Jay, if America could not furnish Spain with Masts and Ship Timber. Mr. Jay replied that those articles might be obtained there. The Count then said that he would defer further remarks on this Head, 'till the arrival of the Person whom he expected

would succeed Mr. Miralles, and appeared desirous of leaving this subject, and, indeed, all other matters relative to American affairs, to be discussed when he came....

Mr. Jay reminded his Excellency in a delicate manner of the Supplies of Clothing etc. etc. [for Washington's troops] which had been promised in a former Conference, and said that if they could be sent in Autumn, they would be essentially useful. The Count assured him that measures would be taken for this purpose, with the Person so often hinted at in the course of the Conference, that probably these Goods would be embarked from Bilboa, as everything was so dear at Cadis. He also once more told Mr. Jay that at all events he might accept the Bills presented by Messieurs Joyce payable at Bilboa—Though he appeared to wish that this measure might be delayed for a fortnight if possible....

In July there occurred an event which helped brighten Jay's drab and discouraging routine of diplomacy and lighten the burdens of enforced residence in an uncongenial and alien land. In an unusually jolly letter, Jay passed on the good news to Sally's father.

Madrid 14 July 1780

I give you Joy—there is a little Stranger here, who I hope will one Day have the Pleasure of calling you Grandfather. On the 9th Instant Sally was delivered of a Daughter as like her Brother as two Children can be. The Mother is in a fair Way and the Child thrives finely. It has as yet no Name nor am I certain what it will be. The old Goody [nurse] has a great Mind to save it from *Limbo* (a Spanish Name for a Dark Receptacle for the Souls of Infants who die unbaptized). About Eight Days ago she presented Mrs. Jay with the Pictures of [here Jay evidently intended to fill in the name of some patron saints, but mailed the letter without finding out which saints they were] Who I presume have succeeded the ancient Goddesses in presiding over Births. If these Saints had any thing to do with it we are much obliged to them, for [Sally] had a fine Time of it.

When the Child was born [the nurse] proposed, as being customary here, to give it the Name of the Saint of that Day—for they are so happy as to have at least one Saint for every Day in the Year. But as the Saints are at War with us Heretics we shall name it after some Sinner that will probably have more affection for it. Wonder on looking over the Almanack I found that the 9th July was the Day of St. Carlo who was a pope, and as neither that Name or office except in the Case of pope Joan ever appertained to a Female I did not see how the old Ladys Advice could be followed in this Instance. I was nevertheless mistaken in supposing this Difficulty insuperable for in similar Cases it seems the Name of *Papa* which is Spanish for pope is taken, as being sufficiently feminine for the most delicate Virgin. However as the popes are as clever as the old Norman Lawyers were in drawing extensive Conclusions from weak premisses, and might possibly from such a Circumstance claim some Right to my little Girl, whom I wish not to embarrass with any Disputes with the See of Rome, I think it will be most prudent to let her take her Chance under the Name of Susanna who was a good Sort of a Woman and nobly resisted the lasivious Attacks of two Inquisitor Generals, whom the Latin Bible have in Compliment I suppose to the Presbyterians stiled *Presbyters*.

I am Dear Sir with sincere Regard
Your most obedient Servant
[JOHN JAY]

The joy was short-lived, as Sally, with tears in her eyes, reported to her "mamma."

Madrid, August 28th 1780

Had I wrote to my dear mamma a fortnight ago while my whole heart overflowed with joy and gratitude for the birth of a lovely daughter, I am sure every line must have conveyed pleasure to the best of parents, who well knows the affection of a mother. Every circumstance united in rendering that event delightful to us—excluded the society of our most intimate friends, behold us in a country, whose customs, language and religion are the very reverse of our own; without connections, without friends; judge then if Heaven could have bestowed a more acceptable present—nor was the present deficient in any thing that was necessary to endear it to us: rather let me say that every wish of my heart was amply answered in the precious gift—in her charming countenance I beheld at once the softened resemblance of her father and absent brother, her little form was perfect symmetry; and nature, by warding off those disorders that generally attack infants, seemed to promise a healthy constitution added to those circumstances, her very name increased my pleasure.... When I used to look at her every idea less pleasant vanished in a moment, scenes of continued and future bliss still rose to view, and while I clasped her to my bosom my happiness appeared compleat. Alas! mamma how frail are all sublunary enjoyments! But I must endeavor to recollect myself.

On Monday the 22nd day after the birth of my little innocent, we perceived that she had a fever, but were not apprehensive of danger until the next day when it was attended with a fit. On Wednesday the convulsions increased, and on Thursday she was the whole day in one continued fit, nor could she close her little eye-lids till Fryday morning the 4th of August at 4 o'Clock, when wearied with pain, the little sufferer found rest in—Excuse my tears—you too mamma have wept on similar occasions. Maternal tenderness causes them to flow, and reason, though it moderates distress, cannot intirely restrain our grief, nor do I think it should be wished. For why should Heaven (in every purpose wise) have endowed it's lovely messenger with so many graces, but to captivate our hearts and excite them by a contemplation on the beloved object of our affection, to rise above those expectations that rather amuse than improve, and extend our views even to those regions of bliss where she has arrived before us—while my mind continues in its present frame: I look upon the tributes my child has paid to nature as the commencement of her immortality, and endeavor to acquiesce in the dispensations of the all-wise disposer of events; and if my heart continues in proper subjection to the divine will, then will she not have sickened, not have dyed in vain.

...Mr. Jay is at present absent, the Court being at St. Ildefonso between 13 and 14 leagues from hence: and I own I never feel so intirely myself as when in his company, for 'tis then that the silent encouragement I receive from his steady, modest virtue, operates most powerfully upon my mind: and I may add upon my conduct; for what can I fear, or how can I repine, when I behold him who is equally interested, composed in danger, resigned in affliction, and even possessing a chearful disposition in every circumstance— excuse me my dear mamma, excuse my officious pen, perhaps too ready to obey the dictates of my heart, but he really is virtue's own self....

I am with the sincerest affection, ever yours
SARAH JAY

During the hot summer of 1780, Jay faced, in addition to his private grief, a horde of creditors of the Congress claiming their pound of flesh. Jay waited with mounting impatience for action from Spain. On August 15, 18, and 25 he wrote Floridablanca reminding him of his acute embarrassment. There was no answer. When Jay called, he was told the Minister was sick, although others had seen Floridablanca that morning. As Jay himself told the Congress, "it appeared to me proper to mention my embarrassments to the French ambassador, who had always been friendly, and ask his advice and aid on the subject." To the Comte de Montmorin, therefore, he related the long and sorry chronicle of his shabby treatment at Floridablanca's hands; then he asked the Frenchman's advice about what he should do.

St. Ildefonso, 27th August 1780

... The Ambassador told Mr. Jay that he ought to ask an Audience of the Minister. To this Mr. Jay replied that he could not hope to have an answer to this request, as he had not been able to procure one to the different applications he had already made.... [The Comte de Montmorin] then asked Mr. Jay, if he had written to Congress, to stop drawing Bills on him. Mr. Jay replied, that he could not with propriety give such information to Congress ... particularly [after] the Minister's declaration that he would be able to furnish him with thirty or forty thousand pounds Sterling at the end of the present or commencement of the next Year, and that in the mean time other arrangements might be taken to pay such Bills as might become due after that Period; He added that if [Floridablanca] had candidly told him that he could not furnish him with Money to pay the Bills, he should then immediately have informed Congress of it, who would have taken of course the proper measures on the Occasion.... [Montmorin] seemed to think the Spanish Minister would pay the Bills that had been already presented....

The Conference ended with a promise of the Count de Montmorin that he would endeavour to speak to the Count de Florida Blanca on the Subject, but that he was afraid he should not be able to do it fully until Wednesday next.

WM. CARMICHAEL, *Secretary.*

Jay, transmitting Carmichael's notes to Congress, added some notes of his own that tell what happened next—and reveal the struggle Jay was having with his own fierce pride and his determination to preserve America's national honor.

... On Wednesday Afternoon the 30th August, I waited on the Ambassador to know the result of the Conversation he had promised to have with the Minister on our Affairs. He did not appear very glad to see me. I asked him whether he had seen the Minister and conversed with him on our affairs. He said he had seen the Minister, but that as Count D'Estaing was present, he had only some general and cursory conversation with him and, slipping away from that Topic, went on to observe that I would do well to write another Letter to the Minister mentioning the number of Letters I had already written, my arrival here, and my desire of a Conference with him. I told the Ambassador that while four Letters on the Subject remained unanswered, it could not be necessary to write a fifth.... I observed to him further, that this Conduct accorded ill with the Ministers assurances; That unless I had met with more tenderness from the Holders of the Bills, they would have been returned noted for non-acceptance. That if such an Event should at last take place after the Repeated promises, and declarations of the Minister, there would of necessity be an End to the Confidence of America in the Court of Spain. He replied that he hoped things would take a more favorable turn, that to his knowledge the Minister had been of late much occupied and perplexed with business, that I ought not to be affected with the Inattention of his Conduct. That ... he would by all means advise me to write the Minister another Letter *praying* an audience.

I answered that the object of my coming to Spain was to make *propositions* not *supplications,* and that I should forbear troubling the Minister with further Letters 'till he should be more disposed to attend to them. That I considered America as being, and to continue Independent in *fact,* and that ... I did not imagine Congress would agree to purchase from Spain the acknowledgment of an undeniable fact, at the Price she demanded for it. That I intended to abide Patiently the fate of the Bills, and should transmit to Congress an Account of all matters relative to them. That I should then write the Minister another letter on the Subject of the Treaty, and if that should be treated with like neglect, or if I should be informed that his Catholic Majesty declined going into that Measure, I should then consider my Business as at an End, and proceed to take the necessary Measures for returning to America....

The Ambassador was at a stand; After a little Pause, he said, he hoped my Mission would have a more agreeable Issue. He asked me if I was content with the conduct of France—I answered most certainly; for that she was spending her blood, as well as treasure for us. This Answer was too general for him. He renewed the question by asking whether I was content with the Conduct of France relative to our proposed Treaty with Spain—I answered that as far as it had come to my knowledge, I was. This required an explanation, and I gave it to him by observing that by the Secret Article [of the Franco-American treaty] Spain was at Liberty to accede to our Treaty with France whenever she pleased, and with such Alterations as both Parties might agree to—That Congress had appointed me to propose this Accession now, and had authorized me to enter into the necessary discussions and Arguments—That to give their Application the better Prospect of Success, they had directed me to request the favorable Interposition of the King of France with the King of Spain; That I had done it by letter to the Count de Vergennes [the French foreign minister], who in Answer had assured me of the King's disposition to comply with the Request of Congress, and informed me that Instructions analogous to this disposition should be given to the Ambassador at Madrid. That it gave me pleasure to acknowledge that his [Montmorin's] Conduct towards me had always been polite and friendly but I still remained ignorant whether any, and what progress had been made in the Mediation.... The Ambassador made no direct reply to these Remarks but again proceeded to repeat his advice that I should try one more letter to the Minister;—I told him, I had after much consideration made up my mind on that Subject, and that it appeared to me inexpedient to follow his advice in this Instance....

How far the tone of this conversation may be judged to have been prudent I know not—It was not assumed, however, but after previous, and mature deliberation. I reflected that we had lost Charleston; That Reports run hard against us, and therefore, that this was no time to clothe oneself with humility.

On considering the Earnestness with which the Ambassador had pressed me to write another Letter to the Minister, I began to suspect that it might be the wish of the Latter, who, conscious of having gone rather too far, might desire this way to retreat through. I concluded therefore to adhere to my Resolution of not writing, but that if the Ambassador should confirm any suspicions by again pressing the measure, in that case to consent to send Wm. Carmichael to the Minister with my compliments, and a Request that he would favor me with a Conference at such Time as might be most convenient to him....

On Saturday Morning the 2d September I committed my Message for the Minister to Mr. Carmichael. ...After being long detained in the Anti-Chamber, he had an opportunity of delivering his Message.... On ... the 3d September Don Diego Gardoqui of Bilboa presented me a Note from the Count de Florida Blanca in these words:

The Count de Florida Blanca presents his compliments to Mr. Jay, and recommends to him to form an acquaintance with the bearer of this Letter, being the Person in question whom he had expected from Day to Day. [Translation]

Meantime Jay poured out his heart to Franklin.

St. Ildefonso 8 September 1780
Dear Sir
...Our Affairs here go on heavily. The Treaty is impeded by the Affair of the Mississippi and the Fate of my Bills is not yet decided. I have been permitted indeed to accept to the amount of about 11,000 Dollars and this Circumstance gives me more Hopes for the Rest than anything else. The Fact is there is little Corn in Egypt. This entre nous.

Charles used the Pardo, nine miles northwest of Madrid, as a hunting lodge. Today it is General Franco's summer home.

Cumberland is here still. His Hopes and Fears are secret. He went from hence a few Days ago and is soon expected back again. To what policy are we to ascribe this. I am told we have nothing to fear. It may be so, but my Faith is seldom very extensive. If we have nothing else to fear we have always Danger to apprehend from such a Spy—so situated, so surrounded by inquisitive communicative and some say friendly Irishmen. In short I wish you could hear me think, but that like most other wishes is vain, and I must leave Time to inform you of many things which at present must not be written....

From Passy came Franklin's reply, containing both sage advice and the promise of financial succor.

Passy, October 2, 1780
Dear Sir:
I received duly and in good Order the several letters you have written to me.... The papers that accompanied them of your writing, gave me the pleasure of seeing the Affairs of our Country in such good Hands, and the Prospect, from your youth, of its having the Service of so able a Minister for a great Number of Years [Jay was then 34, Franklin 74]. But the little success that has attended your late Applications for money mortified me exceedingly; and the Storm of bills which I found coming upon us both, has terrified and vexed me to such a Degree that I have been deprived of sleep, and so much indisposed by continual anxiety, as to be rendered almost incapable of Writing.

At length I got over a reluctance that was almost invincible, and made another Application to the government here for more Money. I drew up and presented a State of Debts and newly-expected Demands, and requested its Aid to extricate me. Judging from your Letters that you were not likely to obtain any thing considerable from your Court, I put down in my estimate the 25,000 dollars drawn upon you, with the same Sum drawn upon me, as what would probably come to me for Payment. I have now the Pleasure to acquaint you that my Memorial was received in the kindest and most friendly Manner, and though the court here is not without its Embarrassments, on Account of money, I was told to make myself easy, for that I should be assisted with what was necessary.... You will not wonder at my loving this good Prince [Louis XVI]: He will win the hearts of all America.

If you are not so fortunate in Spain, continue however the even good Temper you have hitherto manifested. Spain owes us nothing; therefore, whatever friendship she shows us in lending Money or furnishing Cloathing, etca., though not equal to our Wants and Wishes, is however *tant de gagné*; those who have begun to assist us, are more likely to continue than to decline, and we are still so much obliged as their aids amount to. But I hope and am confident, that Court will be wiser than to take Advantage of our Distress.... Poor as we are, yet as I know we shall be rich, I would rather agree with them to buy at a great Price the whole of their right on the Mississippi, than sell a Drop of its Waters. A neighbour might as well ask me to sell my street Door....

I will write to you again shortly and to Mr. Carmichael. I shall now be able to pay up your Salaries compleat for the year; but as Demands unforeseen are continually coming upon me I still retain the expectations you have given me of being reimbursed out of the first remittances you receive.

If you find any Inclination to hug me for the good News of this Letter, I constitute and appoint Mrs. Jay my attorney, to receive in my Behalf your Embraces.

With great and sincere esteem, I have the honour to be, Dear Sir,

Your most obedient and most humble Servant,
B. FRANKLIN

Fortunately, by the time Franklin's reply reached him, Jay's circumstances were not so desperate, for the arrival of Gardoqui, "the person so long expected," seemed to speed up the negotiations with Spain.

Don Diego de Gardoqui was a member of a prominent mercantile firm of Bilbao; one day he would become Spain's first accredited minister to the United States. He began his conversations with Jay by proposing that the United States waive the free navigation of the Mississippi "as consideration for aids." When Jay apprised him that he was not prepared to put that article in question, Gardoqui replied that "the exigencies of state" would not permit the King to pay more bills than the ones which had already been accepted. Jay sought to pin Floridablanca down. Might the United States expect any further aids from Spain?

he asked him in a note written at San Ildefonso on September 14.

Fortuitously, some good news from America arrived overnight. The report of the establishment of the Bank of Pennsylvania and other fiscal efforts of the Continental Congress presented the thirteen states as better credit risks than they had appeared following the fall of Charleston. Jay remarked drily to Congress that it seemed as though America "had risen like a giant refreshed with sleep and doing wonders."

The Spanish court was now ready to make a gesture, but did so with what seems like pathological circumspection. On September 15 Gardoqui turned over to Jay a paper dictated "in his Excellency's name" by Floridablanca's secretary, Don Bernardo del Campo. In substance, it said that the King was prepared to furnish the United States with a credit of $150,000 over a three-year period. The letter was delivered unsigned, and the lawyer in Jay realized that such an anonymous pledge might later be disavowed. It must be signed, Jay insisted, and under pressure Gardoqui agreed to affix his name.

That was the background for the meeting of Jay and Floridablanca held on the evening of September 23, with Gardoqui present as translator. The italicized portions are newly decoded and are published here for the first time.

... Mr. Jay informed his Excellency that the Subjects on which he was desirous of conferring with him arose from the Paper he had received from Mr. Gardoqui the 15th Instant, containing his Excellency's answer to Mr. Jay's letter of the 14th.

Mr. Jay then requested the Count to communicate to His Majesty his thanks for the offer he had been pleased to make of his responsibility in order to facilitate a Loan in favor of America for one hundred and

Louis XVI's warm reception of Franklin at Versailles was a sharp contrast to Charles III's studied neglect of John Jay.

fifty thousand Dollars, and also for the promise of Clothing, etc., etc. and to assure him that the gratitude of the States would always be proportionate to the Obligations conferred upon them. . . .

Mr. Jay resumed his [reference to] the Paper in question, by observing that it assured him it was necessary "That Congress should give sure and effective tokens of a good Correspondence, proposing reciprocal Measures of a compensation etc. In order that his Majesty might extend his further Dispositions towards them." That for his part, he could conceive of no higher tokens which one Nation could give to another of friendship and good will, than their Commissioning and sending a Person for the express purpose of requesting his Majesty to enter into Treaties of Amity and Alliance with them, and that on Terms of Reciprocity of Interest and mutual Advantage. . . . Mr. Jay . . . [remarked] that the Order of conducting that business appeared to him to be this, That as a right was reserved by the Secret Article to his Majesty to accede to the Treaty between France and America whenever he thought proper, and that the Latter would go into a discussion of any alterations the King might propose, that should be founded on reciprocity of Interest. The first question was whether his Majesty would accede to it as it was, or whether he would propose any and what alterations.

The Count here interrupted Mr. Jay by saying that the Interest of France and Spain with respect to America, were so distinct as [to make] different Treaties necessary. Mr. Jay answered that admitting this to be the case, the Treaty with France might be made the Basis, and they might go on Mutatis Mutandis; the Count replied *that his Majesty would never consent to make that Treaty, the basis of one between him and* the United States that *that Treaty* had been *concluded by the French without the knowledge* of the King and *without having made him the offer of being a party to it. That the King's resentment had been so much excited by this conduct* as well *nigh to have occasioned a rupture between* the two Courts, and *that on the secret article being made known to him he* had *answered that when he* found it convenient to *enter into Treaty with the Colonies he would take care of his interest without consulting any one.* Hence he observed it would *not be proper to mention any thing of the French Treaty but to form* one of *anew.* Mr. Jay assured his Excellency that this was the *first time he had ever heard of this Anecdote and expressed some surprise at it.* The Count desired him to *keep it secret adding that the French Ambassador knew it very well.* . . .

[Floridablanca] said that previous to Mr. Jay's or Mr. Gerard's arrival at Madrid, Mr. Miralles had informed him that Congress would yield the Navigation of the Mississippi, but that Mr. Gerard informed him that Congress had changed their resolution on that Subject. . . . The Count . . . made several Observations tending to shew the Importance of this Object to Spain, and its determination to adhere to it, saying with some degree of warmth, that unless Spain could exclude all Nations from the Gulph of Mexico, they might as well admit all; That the King would never relinquish it; That the Minister regarded it as the principal Object to be obtained by the war, and that obtained he should be perfectly Easy whether or no Spain procured any other cession; That he considered it as far more important than the acquisition of Gibraltar. . . .

Shortly thereafter, Jay learned from Gardoqui that Charles III had asked his ambassadors in Holland and France to pass the word that the King was prepared to back whatever loans they might make to America. Jay was prepared for further disillusionment, and his final meeting of the year with Floridablanca, on November 8, only confirmed his suspicion that Spanish efforts to float a loan for America had not been pressed too hard.

Through the year 1781 Spanish-American negotiations sputtered fitfully, and then ground to a halt. Jay's letter to Franklin in Paris remarking that "there is little Corn in Egypt" had correctly reported the negligible financial assistance that Spain stood ready to provide the American rebels. Floridablanca recognized America's potential territorial expansion as posing a threat to that monopolist control of the Mississippi River and of the trade of the Gulf of Mexico that Spain intended to preserve. Accordingly, while doling out a few centavos at a time to relieve Jay's acute embarrassments, Floridablanca kept a tight rein on the purse strings. They would be loosened for Jay, he implied, only if America were prepared to waive her claim to navigate the Mississippi. When the proposition was put to Jay by an agent of Floridablanca, he replied, "The Americans, almost to a man, believe that God Almighty has made that river a highway for the people of the upper country to go to the sea by."

On February 15, 1781, Congress, worn down by backstairs intrigue in Philadelphia, authorized Jay to withdraw his demand for the free navigation of the Mississippi in order to remove the chief obstacle to an alliance with Spain. Jay was not apprised of the revised instructions for many months, and when he received them he prudently made America's relinquishment of the navigation of the Mississippi contingent on Spain's acceptance of an alliance. This was the key proposition Jay put to Floridablanca in Sep-

tember, 1781, but the latter failed to snatch the advantageous offer.

In fact, Spain never made the proposed alliance, nor even presumed to recognize the thirteen states until England had already done so. Actually, therefore, Jay gave up nothing, even though he had to write off further Spanish aid.

In April, 1782, Franklin summoned Jay to Paris.

Passy, April 22, 1782

Dear Sir,

I have undertaken to pay all the Bills of your Acceptance that have come to my knowledge, and I hope in God no more will be drawn upon us, but when Funds are first provided. In that Case your constant Residence at Madrid is no longer so necessary. You may make a Journey either for health or Pleasure without retarding the Progress of a Negociation not yet begun. Here you are greatly wanted, for Messengers begin to come & go, and there is much talk of a Treaty proposed, but I can neither make or agree to Propositions of Peace without the Assistance of my Colleagues. Mr. [John] Adams I am afraid cannot just now leave Holland; Mr. Jefferson is not in Europe, and Mr. Lawrens is a Prisoner, though abroad on Parole.* I wish therefore that you would resolve upon the Journey, and render yourself here as soon as possible. You would be of infinite Service. Spain has taken four Years to consider whether she should treat with us or not. Give her Forty. And let us in the mean time mind our own Business. I have much to communicate to you but chuse to do it *viva voce,* than trust it to Letters. I am ever, my Dear Friend,

Yours most affectionately

B. FRANKLIN

Jay soon prepared to shake the dust of Spain from his boots. Ahead lay the ultimate battles of diplomacy that ended the American Revolution and achieved independence for the Thirteen Colonies. At Paris Jay was to play a stellar role denied him at the court of Spain.

In retrospect, it is doubtful whether anyone could have squeezed more juice out of the Spanish lemon than Mr. Jay. He had managed, with constant nagging, to get Spain to advance the pledged $150,000 over a three-year period. That sum was paid in ten installments to Gardoqui and other Spanish merchant

---

* Thomas Jefferson was among the peace commissioners designated by Congress, but chose not to serve. South Carolina's Henry Laurens had been taken prisoner when Charleston fell to the British in 1780 and transported to England. It was not at all clear to Franklin—even today historians argue the point—whether under the terms of his parole Laurens could properly serve as an American peace commissioner, but he did.

bankers to make good the drafts drawn on Jay by Congress. An additional $24,000 was charged to Jay's account for clothing taken by Spanish ships as prizes from intercepted British vessels and turned over for the use of the American army. By 1792, according to Treasury Secretary Alexander Hamilton's calculations, an additional amount of $99,007.89 was due Spain in interest at five per cent from the date of the loans.

In order to establish American credit Hamilton, without Spain's asking and much to her surprise, borrowed money from the Dutch and paid off the Spanish debt in the fall of 1793. The Spanish government gave receipts, and so the matter ended.

The issue of the free navigation of the Mississippi was not so easily settled. It plagued Spanish-American relations well down into the Washington administration. The problem seemed solved when in 1795 Thomas Pinckney, dispatched on a mission to Spain, obtained from Manuel de Godoy, Spain's principal minister, a treaty by which Spain acknowledged America's western boundary as the Mississippi and conceded both the free navigation of the river and the privilege of deposit of American cargo at New Orleans for a three-year period.

The execution of the treaty was another matter. Several years of disagreeable disputes followed. Spain found one pretext after another to delay evacuating the remaining posts she held on the east side of the Mississippi. Scarcely had a joint survey of the Spanish-American boundary been completed when, in 1800, Louisiana was secretly ceded by Spain to France. Jefferson's purchase of Louisiana from Napoleon in 1803, followed by the Florida purchase in 1819, settled once and for all the issue of the free navigation of the Mississippi and made the United States the master of a great continental domain. The end justified, perhaps, all the forebodings and suspicions of Floridablanca; it also abundantly vindicated the tenacious stand of John Jay back in 1780.

★ ☆ ★ ☆ ★ ☆ ★ ☆ ★ ☆

The excerpt from Lieutenant Kennedy's letter on page 112 reads as follows:

"Thanks for your good wishes on our rescue. We were extremely lucky throughout. After today it won't happen again. Working out of another base—& went in to see the doc about some coral infections I got. He asked me how I got them—I said swimming—he then burst loose with—'Kennedy—you know swimming is forbidden in this area—stay out of the god-damned water.' So now it's an official order—. so no more strain. Best regards to Sted—Red and all the boys—Remember me to Mac if you see him.

Over & out

Jack"

READING, WRITING, AND HISTORY

By J. H. PLUMB

Sympathy for their countrymen in America was widespread among Englishmen on the eve of the Revolution, and it permeated the uppermost layers of British society. Historians, however, have generally underestimated its strength and neglected its causes. In Bruce Catton's regular space in this issue, a distinguished British historian examines a phenomenon which goes far to prove that in the past, as in our own times, public opinion about a foreign war was seldom undivided. Dr. Plumb, a professor at Christ's College, Cambridge, is the author of The First Four Georges *and a contributor to* The American Heritage Book of the Revolution.*
—The Editors*

Doves and Hawks, 1776

On May 20, 1779, the Earl of Pembroke—lord lieutenant of Wiltshire, a former Lord of the Bedchamber to the reigning monarch, George III—was in despair. He felt a deep sense of shame that was impossible to hide. As he wrote to his son, Lord Herbert, who was making the Grand Tour in Italy: "I wish I were a Laplander, or anything but a Briton."

A month later he explained at greater length to his son the reasons for his dissatisfaction:

Our Ministry, taken en gros, are certainly such as no wise nor honest man can trust, & in whom the country can conceive no hopes; men who have proved themselves incapable, whose characteristic is indolence, & whose sistem is unwise, who are overpowered by misfortune, because they are leagued with absurdity, whose obstinacy is not to be softened by advice, & whose eyes are not to be opened by experience.

As a soldier (he was an over-age colonel in the elite Royals) Pembroke was of course distressed by the defeats sustained by the British forces in America—hence his shame—but his anger with the government welled from deeper springs than this. In his quick-tempered, completely uninhibited letters to his son, he does not disguise his contempt for the members of George III's Parliament. He considered it an utterly corrupt institution and he wondered that the people did not nail up the doors of both Houses and set fire to them. In all cities, he told his son, there was the utmost discontent, particularly among manufacturers. His sympathy was with them.

Indeed the political state of England in 1779 was a sorry mess, and for nearly two decades every ministry had proved itself totally incapable of dealing with the American question. During the sixties, harshness alternated with weakness, repression was followed by conciliation as one Whig ministry rapidly followed another. The House of Commons was composed of small Whig factions struggling for power, and George III's faith in Lord North derived from the fact that North in 1770 had brought to an end the confusion of a decade and created a stable ministry, solidly Whig at the core, but supported by many Tories and independents. Nevertheless, not until rebellion flared up was North's American policy much more consistent than that of his predecessors. As rebellion turned to war and the war itself grew long and difficult, many of

97

North's erstwhile supporters began to have doubts of the wisdom of his policy. Criticism grew in volume. And criticism mattered. Public opinion was important in a crisis, even in the oligarchical structure of British politics. Since the accession of George III in 1760, the feeling had steadily strengthened that a Parliament of landowners, dominated by the aristocracy, was becoming out of touch with the true needs of the nation. Criticism of the parliamentary system as well as of North's American policy had become widespread. The radicalism of these critics was social, legal, and religious; not, of course, economic. They believed in a wider democratic franchise, toleration of religious belief, and the rationalization of law and administration. This attitude was particularly powerful among the radical intellectuals and publicists: Joseph Priestley, Richard Price, Thomas Paine, and Junius—that savage critic of George III who still retains his anonymity. Their books and pamphlets were read as eagerly in the provinces as in London, and they had helped to make the American question a burning issue not only for members of Parliament, or even for parliamentary electors, but for all who could read. They appealed particularly to that mass of Englishmen who were politically dispossessed by the quaint franchises of the unreformed House of Commons and who, therefore, felt a natural kinship with the Americans in revolt.

This radical sympathy for America is nowhere reflected so sharply as in Sylas Neville's *Diary*. Neville, probably the illegitimate son of an aristocrat, lived insecurely on the fringes of eighteenth-century social and intellectual life, drifting from London to East Anglia to Scotland, where he finally qualified as a doctor, and then back to Norwich, where he died in 1840. His diary, like Lord Pembroke's papers, is a comparatively recent discovery and one that has passed almost unnoticed by the political historians of George III's reign. For those who believe that radical public opinion mattered little in the eighteenth century, it is an uncomfortable document. Here are a few of Neville's sentiments culled from 1767:

[No] person is a true friend of Liberty that is not a Republican.

The evils of which monarchy is productive should deter any wise nation from submitting to that accursed government.

The Gazette says 10,000 people a year go from the North of Ireland to America and 40,000 in all. May they flourish and set up in due time a glorious free government in the country which may serve as a retreat to those Free men who may survive the final ruin of Liberty in this Country; an event which I am afraid is at no great distance.

Such sentiments would have done credit to a Boston radical, but these were not peculiar to Neville and his friends: they found their echoes elsewhere.

Neville was in touch with many like-minded men and women; some were well-known London radicals such as Mrs. Catharine Macaulay, the Whig historian who enraged Dr. Johnson; Caleb Fleming, the Unitarian minister of Pinners Hall; and Thomas Hollis, whose lavish patronage of liberal ideas helped to keep republican sentiment alive in the middle decades of the eighteenth century. These ardent radical intellectuals certainly fortified Neville's attitude.

Even more impressive, however, are the chance conversations that Neville had, or overheard, which indicate the width of public criticism and the frequency with which it was expressed. At Terry's Coffee House in August, 1768, he got into conversation with a stranger who said that he "wished N. America may become free & independent, that it may be an asylum to those Englishmen who have spirit & virtue enough to leave their country, when it submits to domestic or foreign Tyranny."

At Birmingham, a rapidly growing manufacturing town in the West Midlands of England, a group of professional men, manufacturers, and dilettantes had come together for the purpose of discussion and mutual improvement. They went by the name Lunar Society because they convened on the night of the full moon, which eased the dangers of travel on eighteenth-century roads full of pitfalls and alive with highwaymen. These men had been fascinated by the ideas of the Enlightenment, as indeed had many similar intellectual elites from Philadelphia to Marseilles. The importance of such groups—and particularly the British ones which existed in most large provincial towns—is that they represent not people outside the mainstream of economic and social development but those right in the heart of it. This is certainly true of the West Midlands group, largely based in Birmingham. Their names are well known—James Watt, the inventor; Matthew Boulton, whose great factory at Soho, Birmingham, which made almost anything from steel buttons to steam engines, was one of the marvels of Europe; Erasmus Darwin, grandfather of Charles, poet, philosopher, doctor; Joseph Priestley, who discovered oxygen without knowing it (and whose renown as a chemist, religious teacher, historian, and philosopher was as great in America, where he ultimately died, as in England); Dr. Small, who had tutored Thomas Jefferson in scientific studies at William and Mary College; Thomas Day and Richard Edgeworth, both deeply preoccupied with new theories of education and both weirdly eccentric; and, perhaps the most interesting of them all, Josiah Wedgwood, the potter.

Wedgwood, a man of vast intellectual appetite and broad human sympathy, makes a strong contrast to the drifting and feckless Neville. Everything that Wedgwood did succeeded, and he rose from obscurity to international renown. He was happily married, blessed with brilliant children, prosperous, secure, the admired and admiring friend of many distinguished men in all walks of eighteenth-century life. He certainly cannot be dismissed as a social misfit, as an unkind critic might dismiss Neville, nor can he be lumped together with Price, Priestley, Mrs. Macaulay, and the rest as a disgruntled, radical intellectual. He was a supremely successful man of affairs. He and his friends would have been thoroughly at home in the purposeful, expanding world of Benjamin Franklin's Philadelphia. As with Philadelphia's elite, so with the Lunar Society: its members felt the future in their bones. They were ready for a new world, freer from tradition, closer to the rational principles upon which they modelled their industry and commerce. In general, the Lunar Society members felt as Wedgwood did.

Wedgwood's views on the American problem were conveyed in his letters to Thomas Bentley, his partner, whose judgment—in politics as well as in the arts, sciences, and social intercourse—he revered. Wedgwood and Bentley were, of course, wholehearted supporters of the American cause. They thought coercive measures wicked, preposterous, and doomed to disaster. Wedgwood sent for Dr. Richard Price's *Observations on the Nature of Civil Liberty*. He wrote back enthusiastically:

I thank you for Dr. Prices most excellent Pamphlet. Those who are neither converted, nor frightened into a better way of thinking by reading this excellent & alarming Book may be given up as harden'd Sinners, beyond the reach of conviction.

He asked for more copies so that he could distribute them in the right places. Later Bentley sent him Paine's *Common Sense* and many other pro-American pamphlets to fortify, if fortification were needed, his strong sympathies for America and to help in Wedgwood's work of conversion of others. Wedgwood willingly subscribed twenty pounds toward alleviating the miseries of American prisoners captured by the British.

Of course, it is not surprising that many of the leaders of the Industrial Revolution should have been so strongly pro-American: they too wanted a social revolution, an end to the system of oligarchy and patronage that created not only a sense of keen injustice but also real practical obstacles to their industrial activities. Whatever they wanted—a canal, improved roads, efficient lighting or paving of streets, more education, better law and order, or a new water supply—they had to struggle to get it for themselves. What is surprising is that these social elites, which were beginning to wield so much economic power, proved in the end to be so weak an ally for the American cause.

This was only partially due to the nature of the oligarchical, unrepresentative British political system of the eighteenth century, which put all effective power into the hands of the landowning classes, for many of the industrialists had contacts with politicians, particularly with those Whigs, led by the Marquess of Rockingham and Edmund Burke, who opposed Lord North. The widespread sympathy for America failed to be effective for more profound reasons—the changes in the nature of the conflict itself.

In the 1760's friendly support for America could be indulged with a clear conscience. The policy of successive ministries lacked consistency; many acts—particularly the Stamp Act—seemed to be as inimical to British commercial interests as to American; resentment could be shared in common. But American resentment hardened, developed a program, became a revolt so bloody and bitter that, as William Pitt had foreseen, it turned itself into a European war. Doubts clouded sympathy and consciences became uneasy. It required political and moral convictions of a thoroughly radical kind to support unquestioningly the right of the Americans to obtain their independence by any means whatsoever, once rebellion had started to transform itself into war. Indeed this is sharply reflected in Wedgwood's correspondence. On February 6, 1775, he wrote to Bentley:

I do not know how it happens, but a general infatuation seems to be gone forth, & the poor Americans are deemed Rebels, now the Minister has declared them so, by a very great majority wherever I go.

Yet sympathy for America remained extensive and vociferous. At a meeting at Stafford to adopt a Loyal Address in support of the policy of George III toward America, Mr. Woolridge, a London merchant and friend of John Wilkes who had estates in Staffordshire, produced a counterpetition and proposed it so vigorously that, according to Wedgwood, "the Gentlemen were *cut down* & could not answer him . . ."; nevertheless most of them signed the Loyal Address. Woolridge and his friends, not to be outdone, advertised their counterpetition in the local press, and signatures were canvassed in Birmingham, Lichfield, Walsall, and Hanley. Yet Woolridge, not his opponents, proved to be the loser.

The contrast between the effectiveness of merchant radicals in America and merchant radicals in England became quickly apparent. War strengthened the former and weakened the latter. The taking of New York brought the mob out into the streets. "Our people at [Newcastle]," wrote Wedgwood, "were wild with joy," and he was relieved that those stalwarts who refused to illuminate their houses were not attacked. Elsewhere the mob roared their delight at a British victory. War had inflamed the natural xenophobia of the semiliterate, as indeed it did in America, but, whereas in American mob-support the hopeless anger and despair of the dispossessed strengthened radical and revolutionary attitudes toward government and society, in England the reverse process took place. British merchants who worked for the American cause (short of independence) feared an open alliance with the radicals when war brought the real test, not only because the radicals might be victorious, but also because American independence might lead to a ruin of trade.

In America, radicals were able to exploit patriotic sentiment and so wrest the leadership from the more doubtful and conservative northern merchants or southern planters. Loyalists, supporters of conciliation, could be regarded as traitors and treated as such. The radical detestation of aristocracy could be clothed in hatred for British officials and royal servants. The xenophobic moods of the mob could be used to threaten violence against all who suggested compromise. By such means the radical theories of natural rights and of the equality of men, and the belief that all men had a right not only to life, liberty, and the pursuit of happiness but also to overturn and abolish governments that did not grant them, became essentially American; radical attitudes and patriotism were united by the call of war.

In England, war divided radicalism and patriotism, and tainted the support of America with sedition. Tom Paine became not a hero but an anathema, the symbol of a violent, radical traitor. No one had been more constant in his sympathy toward America than Wedgwood, but war brought him doubts. In the summer of 1779 the extension of the war had so denuded Britain of regular troops that the government encouraged its supporters to raise subscriptions to finance regiments in their counties. On August 7, 1779, Wedgwood attended a meeting of the lord lieutenant, sheriff, and gentlemen of Staffordshire: "The meeting was thin but respectable in number," Wedgwood reported, "and its proceedings enlightened only by a trenchant speech by Mr. Eld, a man of eighty who, after complimenting the soldiers on their bravery, went on to say:

In the times of our prosperity & exultation we, the gentlemen of this county, thought ourselves of consequence enough to address the throne, &, with offers of our lives & fortunes, call'd upon our sovereign to pursue the coersive measures already begun in America. In these days of our humiliation & despondency, which should be a time for learning wisdom, I wish we could now think our selves of importance enough to address his majesty once more, & humbly beseech him to grant such terms to his late subjects in America *as freemen may accept*. I have heard of none such being hitherto offer'd to them. Submission without terms—Unconditional submission! are offers for slaves, & those who accept them must be such. I hope & trust we are none of us in love with slavery.

Wedgwood observed that the old man broke off abruptly. He had wished Eld to say more because he was troubled. He read all the arguments that he could in favor of not subscribing, yet they did not carry conviction with him. In the last resort they conflicted with his patriotism:

[I] am not at present fully convinc'd by them, that it is better to fall a prey to a foreign enemy, rather than to defend ourselves under the present ministry. Methinks I would defend the land of my nativity, my family & friends against a foreign foe, where conquest & slavery were inseparable, under any leaders—The best I could get for the moment, & wait for better times to displace an obnoxious minister, & settle domestic affairs, rather than rigidly say, I will be sav'd in my own way, & by people of my own choice, or perish, & perish my country with me. If subscribing would certainly rivet the present ministry in their places, & non-subscribing would as certainly throw them over, the nation at large being in no hazard at the same time from a foreign foe, I should not hesitate a moment what to do—but none of these propositions seem clear to me.

The upsurge of patriotic sentiment that Wedgwood experienced was typical of many men of similar views. But their support in Britain contracted rather than expanded, once the country was involved in a large-scale war.

This proved true of radicalism's best-organized and strongest supporters, the freemen of the City of London. In the mid-seventies they left Lord North's government with no doubt of their sympathy for the American revolution. In 1773, they chose two Americans then in London, Stephen Sayre of Long Island and William Lee of Virginia, to be sheriffs; in 1774, they insisted on their parliamentary candidates signing pledges to support a bill which would have given America the right to elect its own parliament and to tax itself. Naturally the Coercive Acts were denounced; even as late as 1778 London's freemen refused to give public support to the war. Yet even among men as tough-minded as these, there is a marked decline in their pro-American activity after 1776.

Although they had achieved more or less effective control of the corporation of the City of London, and one or two representatives in Parliament, the radicals had no effective political party. But their ineffectiveness is not to be explained either by the upsurge of patriotism or by the incompetence of their political organization. An important cause arose from their total inability to carry any major Whig politician with them.

ord Brougham, a radical himself and a politician with long parliamentary experience, wrote early in the nineteenth century, "Is any man so blind as seriously to believe that, had Mr. Burke and Mr. Fox been ministers of George III, they would have resigned rather than try to put down the Americans?" And it should be remembered that as late as 1778, Charles James Fox spoke in favor of the Declaratory Act, which categorically stated England's right to tax and rule her colonies. The Whigs brought neither consistent action nor consistent policy to the American situation. In 1774, when radical agitation was at its strongest, the Whig leaders in opposition to the government showed the utmost reluctance to concentrate their energies on the problem of America. The Duke of Richmond said he was sick of politics, and Edmund Burke had to convince the Marquess of Rockingham of "the necessity of proceeding regularly, and with your whole force; and that this affair of America is to be taken up as business." Lacking political leadership in Parliament, smeared with antipatriotism, the widespread radical sentiments of the late sixties and early seventies failed, except in the City of London itself, to become a powerful factor in the American Revolution.

In the end, the acceptance by Britain of America's independence was secured by those country gentlemen who had decided every major political issue in Great Britain since the Reformation. The country interest, the independent members who sat in Parliament as knights of the shire, who never spoke in debates and usually voted with the government, finally rebelled for the very same reason that they had given their initial support to George III and Lord North—taxation. Self-interest, the need to lighten their own taxes, to relieve themselves of the costly burden of defending America, had combined with their traditional respect for the Crown and the sovereignty of Parliament to make them tolerant of the ramshackle confusion, the endless contradiction of what passed for American policy in the 1760's and 70's. What broke their spirit was defeat and, more especially, the cost of defeat.

Lord Pembroke's cry that he wished that he were a Laplander or anything but a Briton was the true patriot's cry, wrung from him by his sharp sense of shame at his nation's failure. Indeed patriotic sentiment deeply influenced all British attitudes to the American Revolution—perhaps more than any other factor. It was only to be expected that sympathy toward America should be rarest among those who were content with the fabric of their society—the aristocrats, gentry, government officers, admirals, generals, lawyers, and ecclesiastics, and that it should be strongest among those new men—the industrial and aggressive commercial classes—to whom the future belonged.

Although radicalism, especially in its demands for parliamentary reform, began after 1783 to climb back to respectability under the aegis of William Pitt and William Wilberforce, the revolutionary wars with France reimposed even more markedly the stigma of disloyalty upon it. Demands for political and social equality became seditious: the ancient institutions—monarchy, aristocracy, landed gentry—were sanctified by patriotic gore. And this sanctification took place when the archaic institutions by which Britain was governed—an extraordinary hodgepodge of feudal custom, medieval chartered rights, and Tudor legislation—were becoming ever more inadequate to meet the needs of the rising tide of industrialism. Consequently, when reform came in the nineteenth century, it was piecemeal, *ad hoc,* never radical in any fundamental sense; Britain never enjoyed, as did America and France, the purging joys of a social and political revolution. Hence, a radical attitude to political institutions and social organization was always tainted with disloyalty in England. And perhaps it should be stressed once again that eighteenth and early nineteenth century British radicalism demanded no more than political and social equality; no more, in fact, than Americans were now guaranteed by their Constitution. Such ideas, however, were no longer British; they were alien, Jacobin.

The American Revolution was almost as much a watershed in the development of British society as of American, for it rendered feeble a widespread middle-class intellectual radicalism that was beginning to root itself in many of the socially and commercially aggressive sections of British society. Its failure to develop and grow, its relegation to political insignificance, its exclusion from the heart of British society, was to taint that middle-class radicalism with oddity, eccentricity, social neurosis, and so justify the continuing anti-intellectualism of the British Establishment. And the corollary was to link patriotism with George III, with monarchy no matter how stupid, with aristocracy no matter how incompetent. As a future of social equality and equal opportunity opened for America, Britain became more firmly saddled with its feudal past.

An Artist Draws the Line

sided with Gray in that regard—but also felt that his title placed him in charge of all surveying work, which did not sit well with Gray. Further, Graham thought Bartlett was concerning himself with secondary pursuits—botany, zoology, geology—to the detriment of the project proper. Somehow, despite the high-level bickering that prevailed during July and August, a modicum of survey work was completed between the Rio Grande and Santa Rita.

But while Santa Rita was perfectly situated, it did not provide fresh vegetables for the men or adequate forage for the animals. Signs of scurvy had begun to appear, and Bartlett made a number of forays southward into Mexico in search of supplies.

On one such trip, early in October, the party was well to the south of Santa Cruz when Bartlett began to suffer intense headaches, chills, and fever. Finally, on a portable cot in an adobe cell behind an abandoned store in Ures, he gave himself up to the ravages of typhoid. Oddly, General García Conde himself contracted the disease at about the same time; in his case it was fatal, and his death did not help the joint effort, already weakened by the delays caused by the wrangling on the American team.

Although he did a few sketches of Ures during his recuperation, Bartlett was not strong enough to leave until late December. Even then the doctors advised against an immediate return to field work, so Bartlett, sketching busily and handsomely all the way, set out for the west coast of Mexico, whence he sailed for California and a winter of re-equipping his entourage for a fresh start in the spring. By this time, Gray's survey team had made substantial progress, advancing along the Gila River to a point sixty miles east of the Colorado. There, with supplies running low, they too decided to push for San Diego and a winter's rest.

In March of 1852, Bartlett was in San Francisco to see to matériel, to negotiate some government drafts, and, incidentally, to enjoy the congenial bustle of urban civilization. He made junkets into the countryside and drew whatever he found—gorges, geysers, quicksilver mines. He hired two San Francisco artists, Harrison Eastman and Henry Box Brown, to render some of his field sketches into finished water colors, and further commissioned Brown to go into the upper Sacramento Valley to draw scenes of Indian life there. Brown returned with a sheaf of sketches, including some of the Chin-ohs, an obscure tribelet living in the shadow of Mount Shasta.

Back in San Diego, the outlook was promising. The men were rested. Graham and Gray had been dis-missed on orders from Washington (this in itself, apparent support for the Bartlett-García Conde line). Their duties were assumed by William Emory, who was in El Paso planning the rapid completion of the project.

The boundary commission started east from San Diego late in May. Its first objective was Fort Yuma, at the confluence of the Gila and the Colorado. The going was rough. The rugged pass separating the coastal plain and the interior desert was but a gateway, in Bartlett's words, to a "vast field of barrenness and desolation." The temperature was often above ninety degrees at sunrise. To compound the hardship, one of the party was murdered by two deserters from Fort Yuma, and night-raiding Indians made off with some of the livestock. They made the fort by mid-June, and were happy enough to be there.

The border eastward from San Diego to Fort Yuma had already been surveyed by one of the earlier commissions. Amiel Whipple, who had headed that work, was attached to Bartlett's party and he now set out to finish the sixty miles east from the fort, to the point along the Gila where operations had ceased the previous January. Whipple found that the rugged terrain prevented his men from triangulating (sighting two key points from a third, and then checking two of these from a new position—forming, crablike, a series of cross-country triangles). They worked as best they could, transit after transit, elevation after elevation. It was a tedious, backbreaking job.

But one of Bartlett's longtime dreams had been "to be thrown among the wild tribes of the interior"; he and a small detachment of companions now went on ahead to live with and study the Maricopa and Pima Indians until the engineers caught up. It was during this period that Bartlett did some of his finest work, especially a view of Tucson and some drawings at the Casa Grande ruin near present-day Coolidge, Arizona. Bartlett tried to learn the ruin's origins from the local Indians, but concluded that "all was in obscurity." The natives claimed the buildings were built by Montezuma, but when pressed for information about him, they confessed "they did not know who the devil he was."

In early August, Bartlett pushed through Guadalupe Pass, and instead of making for Santa Rita, detoured to inspect the Casas Grandes of Chihuahua—like those near the Gila, they were "extensive ruins of an old aboriginal race." He and his group of artist-scientist friends took what time they could to sift debris for artifacts, and Bartlett carefully measured and sketched

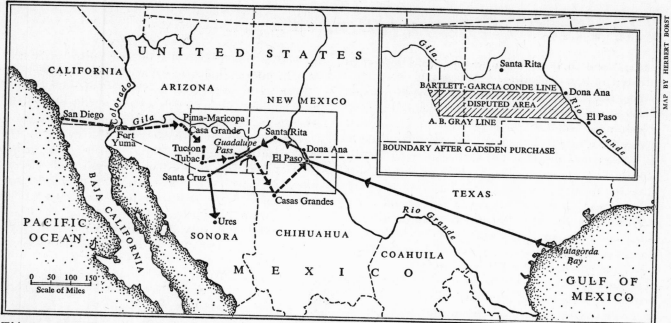

MAP BY HERBERT BORST

This map traces the route of John Russell Bartlett from his arrival at Matagorda Bay late in the summer of 1850 until his departure from the field at the end of 1852. Undelineated are his post-typhoid travels from Ures to Acapulco (where he caught a boat for San Diego), and his junket to San Francisco early in 1852. As the inset shows, Bartlett and Chief Surveyor Andrew Gray disagreed on the boundary's latitude—a dispute that was rendered irrelevant by the Gadsden Purchase of 1854.

details. A good number of villagers turned out to help throw the dirt around, expecting, as Bartlett sourly surmised, "that we should dig out quantities of gold or perhaps Montezuma himself."

Soon after he reached the Rio Grande, Bartlett began to hear of official discontent in Washington. He was being castigated in Congress as a wastrel of public funds, as inefficient, incompetent, and unable to coordinate the project's men and interests. Democratic senators feared that the Bartlett-García Conde line would set back the cause of a transcontinental railroad indefinitely; southern politicians said it would forever preclude a link between the South and California. Soon Congress flatly renounced the line, and demanded the establishment of a boundary no farther north than El Paso. The commissioner decided to return to Washington to defend himself, but with the inauguration the following March of Democrat Franklin Pierce, Bartlett, a Whig appointee, found himself out of a federal job.

Bartlett decided to edit his journal of his boundary years, and it was published in 1854 as the two-volume *Personal Narrative*. A commercial venture—he surely could not hope for government publication—the *Narrative* had a tight budget, and none of the water colors Bartlett had commissioned appeared in it. Nonetheless, it contained ninety-four woodcuts and sixteen lithographs (some Bartlett's, some the work of artists he

hired) and was written in clear, vivid prose that was evocative yet uncluttered by Victorian rhetoric.

When the Gadsden Purchase was ratified in June of 1854, the dispute over the Bartlett-García Conde line became a dead letter, for the area that the former commissioner had supposedly compromised was well above the southern boundary of Mr. Gadsden's acquisition. With the line settled and the political questions removed, the survey work went forward rapidly—under William Emory.

Bartlett thus received little recognition for his years on the boundary, but through his own art and that which he commissioned, he can safely be placed among the best interpreters of the Southwest. Though once the province of a relatively few scholars, Bartlett's work is beginning to receive the wider attention it deserves, as a visual record fascinating in at least three dimensions—art, science, and history.

Robert V. Hine is a professor of history at the University of California at Riverside. This article is based on his book, Bartlett's West, *to be published shortly by the Yale University Press. The bulk of the art that came out of the border survey—both Bartlett's efforts and those of the men he commissioned—has been housed at the John Carter Brown Library in Providence, Rhode Island, with which Bartlett was associated from 1856 until his death thirty years later. The works will be on loan to the Amon Carter Museum in Fort Worth, Texas, for an exhibition that opens this month.*

The Perils of Evangelina CONTINUED FROM PAGE 39

nation," and in every other way possible took steps to cover up his own actions.

The result of the incident was that Evangelina Cisneros was transferred from the Isle of Pines to a prison for women in Havana known as Casa de Recojidas, which had the reputation of being one of the foulest jails in all of Cuba. The inmates, mostly prostitutes, were said to be housed in squalor and subjected to the vilest indignities. But again the facts are thin, the evidence discolored by propaganda.

Thus, with a wide range of controversial material to choose from—and the basic ingredients of melodrama at hand—the subject was a natural for New York's yellow journalists. When the story finally broke in the *Journal* on August 17, it could not help but boost circulation. The *Journal* promised further reports, and for a while the story worked out well. Although nothing further happened to Evangelina, the *Journal* was able to hold its audience spellbound by starting a campaign to enlist supporters for her cause. It urged Americans to send letters and cables to Weyler, to Pope Leo XIII, to the Spanish minister in Washington, and even to Spain's queen regent, María Cristina.

From the opening round, it was evident that the *World* was not going to take this threat to its circulation sitting down. Starting with the printing of Weyler's cable, Pulitzer's staff made every effort to discredit the story, to show that its rival was guilty of gross exaggeration and outright misrepresentation of the facts. The attempt might have succeeded had not the *Journal*, well aware of the value of the case, determined to inject some action into the situation.

The senorita had first come to the *Journal*'s attention when one of its top correspondents, George E. Bryson, sent a dispatch to New York from Havana in June of 1897. He had actually made contact with Evangelina at that time, visiting her at the Casa de Recojidas. His apparent ease in arranging to see her would indicate that prison life was not as severe as had been suggested. Rumor had it that Hearst had sent instructions to his man to rescue Evangelina from Recojidas no matter what the cost. Apparently the Spanish military authorities accepted the rumor as true, for they ordered Bryson to leave Cuba. By

the end of July he was back in New York, but he had enough information to promote the next episode.

Even as Bryson's story about the horrors of Recojidas and the plight of Evangelina was breaking that August 17, Hearst was sending another adventurous correspondent into action on the Cuban scene. He was twenty-nine-year-old Karl Decker (pen name, Charles Duval), described as a "brash and fearless young reporter"—just the man to rescue Evangelina and provide the *Journal* with the biggest scoop of the entire Cuban Revolution.

Decker arrived in Cuba during the last week of August, and he was obliged to check in immediately

In these fanciful sketches, Evangelina reads the letter from Decker, drugs her cellmates' coffee, and, incredibly, tries to slip through unsawed bars.

with the American consul general, Fitzhugh Lee, whose cumbersome obligation it was to prevent any kind of incident that would worsen the already badly strained relations between the United States and Spain. Decker's reaction was not what the consulate might have hoped for: one of his first moves was to enlist the assistance of one of the consular clerks, Don Rockwell, along with another American, William B. McDonald, and an able and enthusiastic Cuban, Carlos F. Carbonnell.

By early September the battle was progressing as heatedly in Manhattan as it was in Cuba. Although other New York newspapers chose to ignore the case as a teapot tempest, the *World* continued to harass its rival by painting Evangelina as a temptress. It quoted

Fitzhugh Lee in direct rebuttal to the *Journal*'s statement that Evangelina was imprisoned "among the most depraved Negresses of Havana" and that she was "to be sent in mockery to spend twenty years in a penal servitude that will kill her in a year."

Lee himself, said the *World,* had returned to New York and declared that the Cisneros girl was well fed and clothed, scrubbed no floors, and was subjected to no indignities or cruelties. In fact, said the Consul General, "she would have been pardoned long ago if it had not been for the hubbub created by American newspapers." Furthermore, crowed the *World,* Lee stated emphatically that Evangelina "was implicated in the insurrection on the Isle of Pines" and that "she herself in a note to me acknowledged that fact and stated she was betrayed by an accomplice."

Above are drawings of the senorita and her rescuers on the prison roof, and of the ladder-bridge leading to No. 1 O'Farrill Street and freedom.

The *Journal* ignored these allegations. It could afford to, for by the second week in September it had stirred up an incredible following, and was holding its vast readership like a puppet on strings of suspense. The question of Evangelina's fate seemed more important than whether the Cuban patriots won or lost their fight for liberty. It was far more vital than any of the routine problems on the home front.

The *Journal* did not rely on its front page alone to attract a mass audience. It cabled Weyler, demanding the prisoner's release. It publicized the fact that it was sending letters, telegrams, and cables to prominent people in the United States and Europe, urging them to use whatever tactics they thought most effective in forcing the Spanish government to free

the pretty captive. Interestingly, some of the most prominent recipients of these pleas responded immediately. Americans, especially women, took up the cause. When those of the stature of Julia Ward Howe, Mrs. Jefferson Davis, Clara Barton, and President McKinley's mother responded to the *Journal*'s campaign, Hearst trumpeted, "The women of America will save her yet, in spite of Weyler and the *World.*"

While Hearst and his able band of conspirators were thoroughly confusing the enemy—all the way from Weyler to the Queen Regent, the Pope, and Pulitzer's journalists—Karl Decker was playing a dangerous game of intrigue in Havana. He had made the costly mistake of trying to bribe several Spanish officials, who all but brought about a banishment similar to that which Bryson had undergone a few weeks earlier.

He was thereby in the unenviable position of having to try to plot an escape alone. As he studied the situation, he came upon a surprising fact: there was a vacant house for rent at No. 1 O'Farrill Street, right next to Recojidas and so close that persons leaning out of the top windows of the two buildings could touch hands. Decker immediately instructed two of his colleagues to rent the house for two months. (They were "highly respectable," said landlord Mariano Fernandez later; furthermore, "they paid in advance.")

Decker was already armed with certain valuable facts. He had a plan of the prison, which Bryson had obtained in June; he also had a list of guards and a schedule of their rounds, data on various forms of available transportation, and the name of a man who could obtain a forged passport at a reasonable price. It had also been learned that Evangelina was imprisoned with eleven other females in a section called "New Hall," supposedly reserved for political prisoners, in the upper story—accessible from the prison roof by use of a short ladder or a length of knotted rope. Although it was exceedingly difficult, Decker finally managed to slip a message through, and to obtain an answer. It said, in part:

Can go down from roof with rope. Need opium or morphine to put companions to sleep. Need acid to cut bars of windows. Stand at corner of building, in street. A lighted cigar will tell me to delay. A handkerchief will tell you it is safe. . . .

Decker now studied the plans of the prison and the rooftop of the house he had rented. Although it would be tricky at night, he decided that he and an accomplice could climb onto the roof and bridge the short span across to the roof of Casa de Recojidas. Accordingly, he had Carbonnell procure a short ladder and an eighteen-inch-wide plank, which he then sawed into three sections, each approximately three feet long. These were hinged so that they could be folded, but when opened out they would serve as a solid unit. He also had a short, knotted section of new rope.

On Tuesday, October 5, a friend of Carbonnell managed to obtain permission for a brief visit with Evangelina. He told her that this was the night the escape would be attempted, and gave her one of the key implements in the plot. A guard was watching closely, but it appeared to be nothing more alarming than a package of candy. This was the narcotic for drugging the inmates in New Hall. (As it turned out, Evangelina had also managed to obtain a drug, laudanum, by feigning an acute toothache.)

Shortly after midnight, when everything was quiet, Decker and two accomplices he later identified only as Hernandon and Mallory completed a major step in the plan. Using the makeshift bridge and the knotted rope, Decker reached the window ledge behind which the Cuban girl was waiting. He had decided against acid for attacking the bars, and began filing away furiously with a small hacksaw. After two hours of perspiring work, he was still only a little more than halfway through, and Evangelina was becoming frantic. Several times they had been forced to stop when the girl's cellmates stirred restlessly and showed signs that the drug was wearing off. Finally, Decker decided that they had pushed their luck to the limit. He told Evangelina that he would return at about the same time the following night.

Wednesday evening, the sixth, was hot, oppressive, and still. For a while the night looked promising, as heavy clouds rolled across the sky. Then, around midnight, as the three men were making final preparations, the clouds vanished and a white moon bathed the rooftops in a chalky glow. That of No. 1 O'Farrill Street seemed especially bright.

About 1:30 A.M., the three men placed the ladder in position. Across the rooftop, at Evangelina's window, they could see a small white handkerchief tied to the bars, the signal that everything was in order. The Cuban girl had managed to put laudanum in the coffee of her fellow prisoners, and it had produced the

hoped-for effect. Hernandon crept across the boards first, followed by Mallory and Decker.

Down on the street, about half a block away, was the shadowy figure of Carlos Carbonnell, casually lounging alongside a carriage. He was to keep an eye on the guard at the entrance gate to Recojidas and later, if the efforts were successful, to whisk Evangelina away in the carriage. Just as the three men reached the roof of the prison, Decker froze. Glancing down, as he did every few seconds, he saw Carbonnell hurriedly lighting a cigar—the signal that there was danger. Up on the roof the reporter and his two accomplices flattened themselves against the roof tiles and could feel their hearts pulsing. A chunk of loose cornice had been dislodged and had clattered to the courtyard below, instantly alerting the drowsy guard.

A few days after disembarking in New York (left), Evangelina was introduced to President McKinley. She was so awed she found herself speechless.

But the man had merely walked back and forth a few paces and then slouched back to his post. Carbonnell ground out the cigar, and the work continued.

This time, after only fifteen or twenty minutes of sawing, Decker was able to swing his weight against the bar, snap it "like cheese," and bend it up far enough to permit a body to pass through. He had hardly finished the job when Evangelina pushed her head out. Decker and the others grasped her arms and pulled her quickly through and into the moonlight. Within seconds, they were back across the boards to the relative safety of No. 1 O'Farrill Street. Although they purposely left the boards on the roof, they inadvertently left behind one of their revolvers.

The next step proceeded without incident. Evangelina was draped in a cloak and escorted casually to the carriage. By 3 A.M. she was in hiding in a private home on the outskirts of the city. Despite a house-to-house search by the Spanish military administration, she remained undetected for two and a half days.

Then, on the afternoon of Saturday, October 9, a young *marinero* might have been seen walking with self-consciously long strides toward the waterfront of Havana. This was Evangelina, outfitted in trousers, a blue shirt with a butterfly tie, and a large slouch hat; she was puffing on a huge dark cigar. Some thirty paces behind her, trying to look unconcerned, walked Karl Decker and one of his accomplices, each concealing a fully loaded Smith & Wesson revolver.

In her pocket, Evangelina carried forged papers identifying her as Juan Sola, and the necessary ticket and documents for embarking on the liner *Seneca,* anchored offshore. At the dock, she calmly boarded the launch that would take her to the ship. Decker and his companion settled themselves nervously at the Café Luz and ordered a round of drinks. The dock area was crowded with Spanish soldiers and officers; Decker was particularly concerned about two military inspectors at dockside. At the very last minute, the engine of the launch refused to start. While the bosun swore and fumed, the inspectors walked over to see what was the matter. Decker's right hand reached for the pistol under his jacket. But Juan Sola, perched by the forward rail, did not seem upset.

An hour or so later, as the lights were beginning to go on around the harbor, the launch chugged out to the *Seneca.* Decker watched the girl as she disappeared onto the deck of the steamer, then returned to his hotel, all but unnerved by the suspense. When he finally heard the ship's departure whistle, he was once again able to relax and begin making plans for his own escape. Eventually he got out of Cuba safely —and aboard a Spanish ship at that.*

The *Journal* saw to it that the arrival of Evangelina Cosio y Cisneros in New York was a great event. The docks were jammed with the curious, as well as with important people who had backed the Cisneros cause. Evangelina was hustled to a large suite in the Waldorf-Astoria, where she was kept in seclusion by the *Journal* just long enough to build up the suspense and prepare for the great climax: a parade to Madison Square, where even the conservative *New York Times* estimated the swarming crowd at 75,000. Mayoral candidate Henry George spoke eloquently about the Cuban cause. Afterward, Senorita Cisneros was acclaimed at a dinner at Delmonico's and later at a ball in the Waldorf's Red Room.

The *Journal*'s final coup was to have its heroine escorted to Washington by her savior, Karl Decker, for an audience with President McKinley.

Throughout the affair, the exasperated editors of the *World* tried vainly to treat the matter as a promotional stunt on the part of its rival, wildly exaggerated and partially fictionalized. But few people paid any attention to the *World*. Why should they, when the escaped prisoner was so beautiful, the cause so worthy, and the rescue so daring?

Trying to maintain some degree of rationality, the *Times* commented, "We do not intend to express any horror or indignation over the lawless act of our contemporary, the *Journal,* in taking Evangelina Cosio y Cisneros from a Cuban prison," thus making its point that Hearst and his men had acted rashly and in a manner not altogether in keeping with international protocol. Nevertheless, it was forced to add, "everybody not entirely destitute of human sympathy is glad, and properly glad, that the girl is free."

For Evangelina Cisneros, overwhelmingly confused by the strange workings of American journalism, the affair ended happily. On June 9, 1898, she was married in Baltimore to Carlos Carbonnell, the Cuban who had played such a vital part in her rescue. After a reception at the Hotel Rennert, "the happy couple left for Washington an hour later."

By then, however, Evangelina was little more than an entry in the closed files of the *Journal*'s past successes. For on February 15, 1898, an event of more than journalistic importance had taken place in the harbor of Havana. With the explosion of the battleship *Maine* and the loss of 260 American lives, even the most ardent practitioners of yellow journalism no longer had to fabricate events to compete for the fancy of New Yorkers.

---

* There was talk that supposedly loyal guards had been bribed by the Americans. At the moment of Evangelina's sailing, warden José Fernandez and four other prison employees, including Mme. Ana Milan de Bendou, wardress of New Hall, were being held incommunicado for questioning. Karl Decker maintained that although he had tried to bribe the guards originally, he had failed. However, Willis J. Abbot, editor-in-chief of the *Journal* at the time, wrote in an account some thirty-five years later that money bought Evangelina's way out of prison and that much of the elaborateness of the plan was an attempt to cover up and exonerate the guards. It seems unlikely that the world will ever know the full story.

Wilbur Cross, an author and editor living in Bronxville, New York, has written several books, mainly on historical topics. Among them are the American Heritage Junior Library Naval Battles and Heroes, *and* White House Weddings, *published last November by McKay. His sources for this article include Frank Luther Mott's* American Journalism *(Macmillan, 1950), W. A. Swanberg's* Citizen Hearst *(Scribner, 1961), and, of course,* The Story of Evangelina Cisneros, Told by Herself *(Continental, 1897).*

"this filthy ironpot"

CONTINUED FROM PAGE 51

One of our ensigns went on a spree last night, got drunk and did not return to the ship until this morning. He came over the side at 10 A.M. with his head swelled up and face scratched, presenting the appearance of a man who had spent the night elsewhere than in his own bed. He was promptly put under arrest by the Captain as soon as he arrived and I have to stand his watch. I have often thought that it is rather hard that a worthless, good-for-nothing fellow can go on shore, get drunk, and raise the Old Boy generally, then come aboard, be put under arrest and have a good loaf in his comfortable quarters while some other officer who is foolish enough to be a gentleman has to bear the punishment of *his* misdeeds.

July 17—. . . Divine services aboard, conducted by the Captain. He stated to the crew this morning that probably within ten days they would have an opportunity to test the relative strength of this vessel and a fort. Our day of sailing was postponed until tomorrow. We will probably leave in the morning for Mobile. Although I feel confident that all is for the best, yet I cannot but wish that we may go to work at once, finish up the fight and return home.

I find myself constantly wishing I was at home. Visions of my sweet wife and of the happy hours we have spent together constantly attend me. I wish to be with her, to be *always* near her. I begin to think that the whole course of my future life has probably been turned by that sweet girl. I cannot go to sea and leave her at home. She is necessary to my happiness. Be with her I must and will. I think it is unkind to her and unjust to myself to be thus separated. Together we would be happy; but separated we will always be dissatisfied. . . .

July 18—This morning just as we were heaving up our anchor preparatory to starting for Mobile, the fire bell was rung most fiercely, the ship having been discovered to be again on fire. We proceeded as usual in such cases and succeeded in quenching the flames in a short time. The fire initiated in the galley and we were obliged to tear the whole apparatus to pieces, in consequence thereof we have been compelled to eat crackers and cheese all day, having no stove on which to cook any kind of a meal. By the time we have served in the *Manhattan* a few months more I think we will be respectable candidates for admission to the New York Fire Dept. . . .

July 19—We finished coaling ship this afternoon for the second time, got under weigh and steamed up the river to a good anchorage, ready to start at daylight

tomorrow morning, provided the ship does not burn up or sink before that time. This evening at 10:20 we were roused up by the old familiar sound of the beat to "General Quarters," cast loose the battery, and got everything ready for action in ten minutes. . . .

July 20—This morning we got under weigh from Pensacola and started for Mobile. The weather has been squally with heavy rain all day. After rather a boisterous passage of seven hours we came near the flagship of the Blockading Squadron off Mobile about five miles from the beach, in full view of the Rebel steamers plying between it and Mobile. The *Tennessee*'s smokestack is visible over the point on which the fort is situated. She has steam and appears to be quite ready for us. I suppose we will have a nearer view of her.

Fort Morgan looks like a huge pile of sand. We can see the Rebels at work in it quite plainly. All the guns are mounted "en barbette," the casemates being entirely closed by a wall of sand forty feet thick, which the Rebs have thrown up as an additional protection against our shot. It is said that three lines of torpedoes have been sunk across the Channel. If such is the case they are by far the most formidable enemy we will have to contend with and we will probably lose some of our vessels in passing them.

The word "torpedo" (see drawing opposite) then meant what the word "mine" means today. The Confederates had sown a large number of floating mines in the channel leading into Mobile Bay. Most of these were simply kegs of powder armed with firing pins, designed to explode on contact; unfortunately for the Confederate cause, the firing pins in many cases corroded and failed to function. After the action, a number of Union ship captains reported that their ships had struck mines that did not explode. One of the monitors, however, the U.S.S. Tecumseh, *struck a mine whose firing apparatus was in good condition, and the* Tecumseh *was lost.*

We are lying in the open sea and the waves are making a clean break on our decks. Everything is closed airtight. The wardroom is at almost boiling heat. The turret is the only inhabitable part of the ship and the open air is constantly so crowded with officers and men passing up and down that we can scarcely find standing room. . . .

Two other ironclads are expected from New Orleans in a day or two. I suppose the general attack will be postponed awhile after their arrival, and probably much longer, but I think we will try the range of our guns at Fort Morgan within a day or two. . . .

July 21—. . . We got under weigh this morning and

stood in shore to within easy range of Fort Morgan. We can see the Rebs at work quite plainly. The *Tennessee* is in full view, and a rather ugly brute she is. The Rebs have not fired at us at all, and we are quite peaceably disposed for the present. I asked Captain Gherardi [commander of the U.S.S. *Port Royal* and an officer under whom Ely had served previously] this evening to apply for me to come aboard his vessel, that I might get out of this filthy ironpot, as I am perfectly disgusted with her and willing to leave her at once; but he told me that the Admiral would not let him have me, and that I was to be executive of this vessel. I am not at all ambitious for the position. I do not think I would get along with Captain Nicholson, as his first lieutenant. He interferes entirely too much with the executive duty of the ship. I like to carry out orders in my own way, and not be continually plied by hints and suggestions from the Captain, and be obliged to follow out my own ideas in the end after a great deal of fuss about nothing. . . .

For nearly two weeks the Manhattan *and the rest of the Union ships lay at anchor outside Mobile Bay while the remainder of Farragut's assault force assembled. Not until August 4 did the last of his ironclads, the ill-fated* Tecumseh, *arrive on station.*

August 4—The ball was opened this morning by the monitor *Winnebago*. She stood in toward Fort Gaines and opened fire on some Rebel steamers discharging freight at the wharf. She made most miserable shots, and the steamboats did not cast off a line but continued to discharge until they had finished, and then quietly steamed away. Fort Gaines opened on the monitor, and after some rather wild shooting made more tolerable shots. None of them, however, struck the monitor. . . .

The *Bienville* arrived this evening with the Monitor *Tecumseh* in tow. She is a sister ship of this. Rations were cooked today for tomorrow. Signal men from the Army are aboard and we are ready to get under weigh at daylight. We have got our guns to work quite well, and I take the credit to myself—in my own diary—I hope we may be successful and that everything will work well.

August 5—This morning the fleet got under weigh at 6. The *Brooklyn* and *Octarara* led the van, next *Hartford* and *Metacomet* lashed together, next *Richmond* and *Port Royal*, next *Ossipee* and *Itasca*, next *Oneida* and *Galena*, *Lackawanna*, and *Seminole*. The ironclads, four in number, this vessel, the *Tecumseh*, *Winnebago*, and *Chickasaw*, were on the right flank of the fleet attacking in columns and therefore between it and the Rebel Fort Morgan.

The engagement was commenced at 6:45 and lasted until eleven. The *Tecumseh* was blown up by a torpedo within a ship's length of this vessel in the very commencement of the engagement. She sank in seven minutes, and only one ensign, the pilot, and four men were saved from her. The whole of the balance of the officers and men went down in her.

The battle was terrific, the most severe naval engagement of the war. We came within close point-blank range of the forts, and they threw a perfect storm of shot, shell, and grape. Our loss in killed and wounded was nearly 300, a very heavy proportion for the small number of persons exposed in the fighting decks to the enemies' fire. After passing the forts we engaged the Rebel fleet of four vessels, capturing the *Selma*, sinking the *Morgan*, and capturing the *Tennessee*, who struck to the *Manhattan*.

I put two 15-inch solid shot through her and the Captain put one. We had the guns out and I had

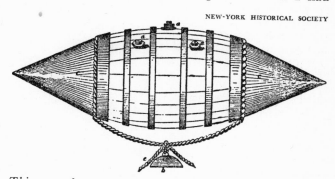

NEW-YORK HISTORICAL SOCIETY

This was the type of "torpedo" that sank the monitor Tecumseh. *Ordinary lager beer barrels were confiscated throughout the Confederacy. Engineers had them securely calked, loaded with gunpowder, fitted with friction fuses, and then moored in a line across a navigable channel.*

given the order "Ready!" Our vessel [was] within 50 yards of her and going at full speed. I was about to give the order "Fire!" which would have sent 870 pounds of cold iron fore and aft the whole length of her gun deck, when the Captain called out to me not to fire, that "she had surrendered."

We all jumped out on deck, and sure enough the Rebel flag was down, much torn and the pale flag of truce in its place. We stopped the engines at once and just steamed clear of her, having been steaming after her at full speed with the intention of ramming her as we fired the last shot. The Captain ordered me to board her and take her colors, which I did.

Her decks looked like a butcher shop. One man had been struck by the fragments of one of our 15-inch shot, and was cut into pieces so small that the largest would not have weighed 2 lbs. The Rebel Admiral was wounded. None of us was hurt.

In the heat of the action, Lieutenant Ely seems to have gotten a few of its details scrambled. Farragut actually steamed into battle with fourteen wooden ships; besides those Ely named, the Monongahela *and the* Kennebec *were on hand. For a more accurate account of the* Tecumseh's *sinking and the fate of her crew, see page 51. Finally, Ely seems to have overestimated the damage done by* Manhattan's *15-inch guns.* Tennessee's *armor was not penetrated. One of Manhattan's shot, however, did buckle the ram's armor and splinter the wooden backing, so that another shot in the same place would probably have gone through. In addition,* Tennessee's *bow and stern guns were put out of action because the Federal pounding jammed the iron gun ports and made it impossible to open them. The dreadfully dismembered sailor mentioned by Ely came to his end when a solid shot arrived just as he was trying to repair one of those gun ports.*

August 6—We lay very comfortably all night, not having been bothered by the Rebel torpedoes. This morning the U.S.S. *Metacomet* went out with the wounded under a flag of truce, bound for Pensacola. The Rebel commander of Fort Morgan, Maj. Gen. Richard L. Page, gave the Admiral permission to send her, provided "she returned," as he said "he had us now just where he wanted us." I think he will want us away again before he gets through with us. A blockade runner managed to get past us in the night and arrived safely at Mobile.

This morning we found that Fort Powell had been evacuated and the magazine blown up in consequence of the fire from one of our monitors. The monitor *Winnebago* went in and engaged Fort Gaines this afternoon, making some splendid shots, and only receiving one in return. On Monday we are to join in with the other ironclads and see if we can drive the Rebels out of it.

August 7—This morning a general order from the Admiral, expressing his thanks to the officers and men of the different vessels of the fleet which participated in the fight of the 5th, was read on the quarterdeck at general muster, also an order for the fleet to return thanks to Almighty God for the victory gained by us on that day....

A Rebel flag of truce boat came down from Fort Gaines this morning with proposals of capitulation from the Rebel commanding officer there, stipulating for the surrender of the place, the Rebels marching out with the honors of war. They wish to surrender to the fleet, in preference to being stormed out and compelled to surrender to the Negro troops now investing the place. I understand that the Admiral demands unconditional surrender. I [also] understand that I have been recommended by the Captain for promotion in consideration of services rendered in the late engagement.

August 8—This morning at 10 o'clock Fort Gaines surrendered unconditionally to the naval forces of the United States stationed in Mobile Bay. We captured 850 prisoners of war.

Fort Morgan still lurks in sullen silence. I imagine we will soon be sent in to wake them up and try once more what we can do with them. It is finally supposed that our work here is almost accomplished. When Morgan surrenders, four vessels can blockade the harbor of Mobile and the balance of the fleet can be removed to wherever it will be most needed. We are to go to Pensacola to refit. From thence we will proceed to New Orleans, lay back on our laurels and have a good time generally. I propose to apply for a leave of absence.

August 9—This morning we got under weigh at 10 and steamed in to engage Fort Morgan. The action commenced at 11. We threw in 15 shells from this vessel, twelve of which burst directly *in* the fort, and three others on the parapet. The Captain said I made the best artillery practice he ever saw. We were struck several times, and one bolt head struck the Captain in the foot, not breaking the skin. At 1 we ceased firing and stood out toward the fleet. At 3 we stood in to renew the engagement but got aground, and through the stupidity of those who attempted to haul us off, we remained stuck until 10 at night, within close range of the fort; but we received no injury. We came to again at 10:30 a mile from the fort.

August 9—We have never heretofore appreciated the risk we ran in our attack on Forts Morgan and Gaines. Rebel officers inform us that we passed over 300 torpedoes in our course. We knew that the channel was full of them, but the Admiral acted upon the belief that they had been submerged so long that a great part of them would not explode, and fortunately his surmise proved correct. The ships, in cruising in, heard the continued snapping and pinging of those infernal machines, but the powder proved to be inferior, and although the percussion exploded, the torpedoes remained harmless. The one which blew up the *Tecumseh* had been planted that very morning.

August 10—We have been lying quietly all day within seventeen thousand yards of Fort Morgan. We have exchanged no shots, but have mutually kept a bright lookout.... The bombardment will probably commence again tomorrow.

I am very much disappointed at not receiving a word from Nellie. I will not believe that she has not written. I hope she is well. This silence is unaccountable. We have suffered excessively from the heat

a truthful sketch of the Manhattan as she was when I visited her this morning —

This sketch of the Manhattan *was drawn by one Robert Walter Weir, Jr., who visited the ship just before the battle.*

in the wardroom all day. Everything is closed up tight and as it is raining it is impossible to get fresh air without getting wet also.

August 21—I have been suffering perfect torture since [August 12] with my right arm, having had a most painful swelling on the joint, caused by a contusion received on the 5th ult. I have resumed my duties today, and with them my journal. We have been paying our respects to the Rebels in Fort Morgan with great regularity.

Yesterday morning, as I felt a little better, I took charge of the battery. They had been firing on the lighthouse which the Rebels used as a kind of citadel. The Captain asked me if I could knock it down. I told him I would try. The first shot was a little to the right of it, making some ugly scars. The next struck it fair and square and one half of the whole building came tumbling down about their ears, raising a perfect cloud of brick dust. I felt proud but rubbed my arm all the time.

August 22—A steady bombardment all day from our ironclads, all bearing on Fort Morgan. We have picked it pretty well to pieces. The shells strike beautifully. We have penetrated this citadel. The guns work beautifully and bright this morning, as we watch their flying course through the heavens in their huge arc and then mark the massive glare of their explosion. After a hard day's fighting I don't feel much like writing.

I received a very nice letter from Nellie. God bless her! I *do* believe she loves me.

August 23—At 4 A.M. we got under weigh, cleared ship for action, and stood down toward Fort Morgan, to commence the bombardment for the day. At 6, just as we had arrived at the place "of fight," some one "sang out" a flag of truce from the fort! Of course glasses and bare eyes were at once turned in that direction, and sure enough there we saw the white flag waved once more in Mobile Bay.

The fort had been set on fire the night before by one of our shells and had been burning furiously all night, the flames lighting up the whole southern part of the bay and making quite a pretty spectacle. We all remained on deck after we had ceased firing

[illegible word follows] watching the conflagration and the higher streaks of flame flying through the air, which marked the tracks of the mortar shells (twelve inch) fired without ceasing by the Army during the whole night. At 4 A.M. the fort was set on fire in another place by those projectiles, the whole interior of the fort being in a blaze and making it so hot within the works (180°) that the Rebs had to "come down" and cry enough.

At 2 P.M. I went on shore with the Captain and watched the ceremony of the surrender to the combined naval and military forces of the United States. The greybacks marched out without music, formed a line on the beach and stacked arms, surrendering themselves unconditionally, as prisoners of war. Our boys then marched up to the tune of the Star-Spangled Banner, with colors flying, formed a line in front of the Rebs and said "Where are your leaders?" This is truly the thrilling part of war. The Rebel flag was hauled down and the Stars and Stripes hoisted over Fort Morgan at 2:20, the fleet and the army both saluting the glorious old flag as it was run up.

We then went into the fort and found it well battered, but one gun was left uninjured in the whole fort. The citadel was completely destroyed. The Rebs said that one of our 12-inch shells penetrated the parapet, pierced the citadel through and through and buried itself fifteen feet in the sand, but did not explode. Had it done so, they said that it would have killed or wounded half the garrison, as they were all in the citadel at the time.

With the surrender of Fort Morgan, the 1864 operation against Mobile Bay came to an effective close; no attempt was made at that time to take the city of Mobile itself, twenty miles farther up the bay—with the destruction of the Confederate fleet and the capture of the forts the Union forces had effectively closed the port to blockade runners, and the city itself was not taken until the following spring, when the war was coming to an end.

On August 26, Lieutenant Ely became executive officer of the Manhattan, *and a few weeks later he was promoted from acting lieutenant to lieutenant. Before the battle he had had an argument with his skipper, Commander Nicholson, but it seems to have left no soreness, and by October 6 Ely was writing: "I like him better than any commanding officer with whom I have sailed. I was not at all prepossessed with him at the time of my entry upon my present duties, but I have found him up to this time most reasonable." Three weeks later the young lieutenant noted happily that he had been recommended for promotion to lieutenant commander.*

"But don't go near  *the water"*

The following is the last paragraph of a letter written in October, 1943, to Lieutenant Patrick Munroe, U.S.N.R. It came from a friend who, like Lieutenant Munroe, was the commander of a PT boat in the South Pacific.

Thanks for your good wishes on our rescue. We were extremely lucky throughout. After today it won't happen again. Working out of another base — & went in to see the doc about some coral infections I got. He asked me how I got them — I said swimming — he then burst loose with — "Kennedy — you know swimming is forbidden in ~~this~~ ~~this~~ this area — stay out of the god-damned water." So now it's an official order — so no more Oltai. Best regards to Sled — Red and all the boys — Remember me to Mac if you see him.

I won't not

Jack.

(*Reproduced with the permission of Mrs. John F. Kennedy and of Mr. Patrick Munroe. For a printed version of the paragraph, see page 96.*)